EDITED BY
KAREN WINTER AND GILLIAN RUCH

SUPPORTING YOUNG CHILDREN'S PARTICIPATION IN CHILD WELFARE

European Perspectives

POLICY PRESS SHORTS POLICY & PRACTICE

First published in Great Britain in 2025 by

Policy Press, an imprint of
Bristol University Press
University of Bristol
1-9 Old Park Hill
Bristol
BS2 8BB
UK
t: +44 (0)117 374 6645
e: bup-info@bristol.ac.uk

Details of international sales and distribution partners are available at
policy.bristoluniversitypress.co.uk

© Karen Winter and Gillian Ruch 2025

The digital PDF and ePub versions of this title are available open access and distributed under the terms of the Creative Commons Attribution-NonCommercial-NoDerivatives 4.0 International licence (https://creativecommons.org/licenses/by-nc-nd/4.0/) which permits reproduction and distribution for non-commercial use without further permission provided the original work is attributed.

British Library Cataloguing in Publication Data
A catalogue record for this book is available from the British Library

ISBN 978-1-4473-7603-3 paperback
ISBN 978-1-4473-7604-0 ePub
ISBN 978-1-4473-7605-7 OA Pdf

The right of Karen Winter and Gillian Ruch to be identified as editors of this work has been asserted by them in accordance with the Copyright, Designs and Patents Act 1988.

All rights reserved: no part of this publication may be reproduced, stored in a retrieval system, or transmitted in any form or by any means, electronic, mechanical, photocopying, recording, or otherwise without the prior permission of Bristol University Press.

Every reasonable effort has been made to obtain permission to reproduce copyrighted material. If, however, anyone knows of an oversight, please contact the publisher.

The statements and opinions contained within this publication are solely those of the editors and contributors and not of the University of Bristol or Bristol University Press. The University of Bristol and Bristol University Press disclaim responsibility for any injury to persons or property resulting from any material published in this publication.

Bristol University Press and Policy Press work to counter discrimination on grounds of gender, race, disability, age and sexuality.

Cover design: Kitty Russell
Front cover image: Shutterstock/Strejman

This book is dedicated to Manuel Ortíz Mateos, a member of the PANDA team and an inspiration to all who knew him. Manuel contributed a chapter to this book and sadly died before the book was published. We remember his kind, gentle and thoughtful approach and his unwavering commitment to social justice, equality and human rights, as manifested in his participation work with the Roma population in southeast Madrid, Spain.

Contents

List of figures, tables and boxes		vi
Notes on contributors		viii
Acknowledgements		xii
Foreword by Gillian Ruch		xiii
Preface		xv
one	Introduction *Wendy Eerdekens and Karen Winter*	1
two	Young children's rights *Karen Winter*	16
three	Contextual influences on participation *Wendy Eerdekens, Eva Heirbaut, Karen Winter, Alicia Toal, Geraldine McGuigan, Carmen Roncal Vargas, Manuel Ortíz Mateos, Inger Sofie Dahlø Husby and Randi Juul*	33
four	The participation rights of infants and babies *Wendy Eerdekens and Eva Heirbaut*	54
five	Creative participatory approaches, methods and tools *Esther Mercado Garcia and Elin Hassel Iversen*	71
six	Listening and talking to young children outdoors *Inger Sofie Dahlø Husby, Pål Børmark and Solvår Hernes*	98
seven	Key principles in participation and collaboration with young children *Karen Winter and Gillian Ruch*	117
Index		124

List of figures, tables and boxes

Figures
2.1	The four foundational pillars of the UNCRC	18
2.2	The interrelated UNCRC articles that define children's participation rights	19
5.1	A home therapeutic sand tray for individual use over time	77
5.2	Teater Fusentast: performing in a box	80
5.3	Teater Fusentast: inside the box	81
5.4	Methodological 'pieces' of the Mosaic approach	83
5.5	Image theatre work session at Ørland kulturskole, Norway	84
5.6	Children in theatre	84
5.7	Peacepainting	87
5.8	Half water and half lava	88
5.9	Change processes in painting workshops	89
6.1	Decoration	105
6.2	Two boys on an outdoor walk	110

Tables
1.1	PANDA project members	6
2.1	Best practice principles in working with children	30
4.1	Practice tips for ensuring that the voices of babies and infants are heard and considered	67

Boxes
4.1	Social worker observing baby Sam (six months old) in a nursery setting	62
4.2	Social worker positioning baby Sam at the centre of a meeting involving parents	63

5.1	Professional playfulness with children	72
5.2	Puppets in practice	79
6.1	Ten-year-old Ann	100
6.2	Engaging Ann in outdoor activities to facilitate communication	102

Notes on contributors

Pål Børmark is a clinical family therapist and head of clinical practice in children and family services at the LINK Care Unit, Municipality of Trondheim, Norway. He holds a bachelor's degree in social work and works directly with children and young people.

Wendy Eerdekens is a lecturer and researcher at Artevelde University of Applied Science in Ghent, Belgium. She is a social worker, a qualified system and family therapist, and a supervisor. She has 19 years of field experience in youth care and mental healthcare with children and families. The focus of her research and teaching is mainly methods in social work and the voice of children, youngsters and parents in youth care and the broader field of social work.

Esther Mercado García is a reader/professor at Complutense University of Madrid, Spain with a PhD in social work. She is a social worker and family therapist accredited by the Spanish National Federation (FEATF). She is also a teaching collaborator at the AVANCES Training Center, specialising in training in family therapy. Her research topics include social work with families and children, social work involving those with intellectual disabilities and mental issues, methodology in social work and qualitative research. She is currently deputy director of the Diversity and Inclusion Unit (Social Policy Delegation) at the Complutense University of Madrid and deputy convenor of the Specialist Interest Group Children's Rights in Practice at the European Association of Research in Social Work (ESWRA).

Eva Heirbaut is a social worker and a certificated contextual therapist. She is a lecturer and researcher at Artevelde University of Applied Science in Ghent, Belgium. She has extended experience in mental healthcare with children, young adults and families. She works as a psychotherapist and family therapist in a multidisciplinary practice and is a trainer in the post-initial course 'systemic and contextual counselling'. Her main research topics are (mental) healthcare and methodical thinking and acting in social work.

Solvår Hernes is a clinical social worker and head of the unit in children and family services at the LINK Care Unit, Municipality of Trondheim, Norway. She holds a master's degree in social work, and works directly with children and young people, as well as having responsibility for the delivery of the service.

Inger Sofie Dahlø Husby is Associate Professor in the Department of Social Work at the Norwegian University of Science and Technology. She holds a bachelor's degree in child protection and child welfare, a master's degree in social work and a PhD in social science with a specialisation in social work. Her research focuses on the interaction between children and child welfare workers, with a particular emphasis on communication, cooperation, trust building and children's participation. She is also a member of the organising team for the Special Interest Group (SIG) on Children's Rights in Practice within the ESWRA.

Elin Hassel Iversen is Assistant Professor at the Norwegian University of Science and Technology, teaching communications and activities using drama pedagogical methods. Her work focuses on the central role of utilising cultural and artistic disciplines as interactive activities for children and youth, as well as creating educational videos and video documentation. She also works as a stage director staging theatre productions with both professional actors and amateurs, including children, youth and adults. In addition, she writes scripts for theatre and develop stage design.

Randi Juul is Associate Professor, teaching and doing research at the Norwegian University of Science and Technology (NTNU) in Trondheim, Norway. Her main topics are child welfare and protection, social pedagogy and communicating with children and parents in the context of child welfare. She has published on topics such as language use and perspectives on children in child welfare, social pedagogy and communication and collaboration with children in child welfare. She also has practical experience of working with children and families in the field of child welfare and protection.

Manuel Ortíz Mateos was an anthropologist and certificated mediator and director of social services centres and programmess. In 2001 he took up a post working for the Fundación Secretariado Gitano (FSG) in Madrid, Spain. He coordinated an intercultural and interdisciplinary team with responsibilities in education, childhood, employment, gender equality, anti-discrimination and participation work with the Roma population in southeast Madrid. Sadly, he died in 2025 shortly before the publication of this book.

Geraldine McGuigan is an area manager in the Voice of Young People in Care (VOYPIC) organisation in Northern Ireland. She has responsibility for the coordination and delivery of services for children in care in these areas.

Gillian Ruch is Professor of Social Work in the Department of Social Work and Social Care at the University of Sussex,

UK. She teaches and researches in the areas of childcare social work and relationship-based and reflective practice, and is committed to enhancing the wellbeing of children, families and practitioners. Her particular interests are in promoting psychosocial research methods and reflective discussion and supervision forums that facilitate relationship-based practice and promote practitioner wellbeing. She co-edited (with Danielle Turney and Adrian Ward) *Relationship-Based Social Work: Getting to the Heart of Practice* (Jessica Kingsley, 2010) and publishes widely on relationship-based and reflective practice.

Alicia Toal is a qualified social worker and chief executive of the Voice of Young People in Care (VOYPIC) organisation in Northern Ireland. She has responsibility for the organisational management of the organisation and represents VOYPIC on several departmental and governmental fora.

Carmen Roncal Vargas works at the Fundación Secretariado Gitano, Madrid, Spain, and is an Associate Professor at the Faculty of Social Work of the Complutense University of Madrid. She holds a PhD in social work and her research interests include team management and organisation analysis, corporate social responsibility, unaccompanied minors, child poverty, child participation, social exclusion and gender perspectives.

Karen Winter is a qualified social worker and Professor of Children's Social Care at Queen's University Belfast, Northern Ireland. Her research interests concern young children in care, their rights, relationships, wellbeing and outcomes. She has published extensively in this area, most recently (with Patrick Thomas) publishing *Social Work with Young People in Care: Looking after Children in Theory and Practice* (Routledge, 2024).

Acknowledgements

The PANDA team wishes to thank the children and young people who gave the project team members permission to attend events that they were involved in and to view resources designed with them. We would also like to thank colleagues who read drafts produced by our chapter contributors and to the wider team who made other invaluable contributions to the project. These include our colleagues Linda Aerts, Nele Haedens, Lisselotte Lowagie and Virna Saenen in Opgroeien (the Growing Up organisation) in Belgium, Paul McCafferty from Queen's University Belfast, and Marta Blanco Carrasco, Ana Isabel Corchado Castillo and Maria Begona Leyra Fatou, from Complutense University of Madrid. Lastly, we would also like to thank the many other people in Norway, Spain, Northern Ireland and Belgium who gave up their time to join us in our learning week in each country and to freely share their ideas, experiences and resources regarding young children's participation with us.

Foreword

Gillian Ruch

PANDA Project consultant and Professor of Social Work, University of Sussex, UK

We are sitting in a room at Artevelde Hogeschool in Ghent, Flanders, listening to the manager of a Family Support Centre describe how he helps an infant, arriving for the first time to receive respite care with them, to feel at home. Although the infant cannot talk yet with fully formed words, the manager describes how he walks around the building with the infant in his arms and talks with the infant, letting them know where they are going to be sleeping and where they will eat with the other children staying at the centre. He relates that every child, even a baby, has the same need for reassurance regardless of their age. His description was immensely poignant as it provided such an intimate insight into the professional practice of the Centre and its attuned approach to help infants feel part of the decisions being made about their lives, even though they are too young to speak.

In my role as a consultant to the PANDA project, I have had the privilege of accompanying the team members for the duration of the project, and this particular practice encounter (outlined above), which took place at the outset of the project, has stayed with me. Over the course of the project's life, each of the four countries represented has provided equally moving examples of thoughtful, child-centred engagement with very young children, based on respect for their worth as humans and aimed at helping them and other children like them participate in the decisions being made about their lives. All this thinking has been firmly rooted in children's rights and the United Nations Convention on the Rights of the Child.

The project team comprising British, Flemish, Norwegian and Spanish social work academics and practitioners have travelled from Flanders, where it began, as far north as Trondheim in Norway, as far south as Madrid in Spain and as far west as Belfast in Northern Ireland. Part of the team's distinctiveness has been its shared value base and the close collaborative working relationships it has forged between practice and academia in each of the four countries. Rooted in real-life practice, the project has stayed close to very young children's lived experiences. The multitude of invaluable artefacts it has curated on the project website (reacch.co.uk) reflect this 'practice near' positioning of all the project's work.

This book represents the culmination of the PANDA project and reflects the riches that the project has generated. We hope that it will be an inspiration for everyone engaged in working professionally with very young children. We trust that it will encourage us all to allow very young children the opportunity to be heard, even when they cannot yet speak with words, and to be noticed and included in everything that concerns their everyday lives. We offer it as an inspiration for us all to hold children in mind in our relationships with them, in all that we do with them and on their behalf.

Preface

When the proposal for the PANDA project was written, the team did not intend to write a book. The idea grew out of a desire to ensure that the ideas, practices and resources gathered during the life of the project could be made available as widely as possible. This desire reflects the team's shared commitment to try and make a difference to very young children by strengthening the awareness of professionals, managers and policy makers of young children's participation rights. While there have been new practice, policy and legal developments in the countries represented in this project, it remains the case that the participation rights of our very youngest children have a way to go in order to be fully realised in daily practice. As such, our main focus has been to produce a text that is accessible, informative and helpful.

Much of this book concerns face-to-face, child-friendly approaches that develop within the context of trusting and meaningful relationships because these remain a core and central aspect of all child welfare and child protection assessment processes. We acknowledge the limitations of the book. In particular, although the project took place during the COVID-19 pandemic, when much practice shifted to online delivery, there has not been the time, space and resources for the PANDA project to consider the impact of digitalisation and the possibilities and opportunities it presents to very young children and the adults caring for them or working with them to realise their participation rights. That said, the book highlights innovative approaches reflecting country-specific contexts and these re-ignited a sense within the team that we were all committed to the same endeavour: making the inaudible voices of very young children audible. We hope your own passion to young children's participation rights is similarly re-ignited.

ONE

Introduction

Wendy Eerdekens and Karen Winter

Introduction

This Policy and Practice Short has emerged from an Erasmus+ Key Action 2 project funded by the European Union (EU) (https://erasmus-plus.ec.europa.eu/programme-guide/part-b/key-action-2). The project has become known as the PANDA project, an acronym drawn from the words *participation and collaboration for action*, and its focus is on promoting the participation rights of young children, aged 12 and under in child welfare and child protection. The project is based on collaborative relationships between academics and professionals involved in child welfare and child protection from eight partners in four nations – Belgium, Northern Ireland, Norway and Spain –and took place between September 2020 and August 2023.

Why the PANDA project?

> A voice for children is very important because it helps promote their self-esteem and their self-worth. I think

> by enabling children to have a voice through choice, by helping them express their views, wishes, feelings and emotions, children learn that they are important and that they are valued, and we can also help to keep them safe.
>
> Toal, *A Voice for Children*, 2022

While much attention has been given to social work and children's rights, and there has been significant progress in law, policy and practice, the participation rights of *very young* children known to and/or in the care of social services remains an ongoing concern across Europe. The views, experiences and perspectives of this group of children (which includes children under 12 years of age and in particular babies and infants) are often overlooked by professionals and decisions are made on their behalf without any active engagement with them. This is concerning because we all share moral, social and legal obligations to respect the worth of each individual child and their views, irrespective of their age and other characteristics, as outlined in the United Nations Convention on the Rights of the Child (UNCRC) and the supporting General Comments, published by the Committee on the Rights of the Child, which give detailed guidance on implementation of the specific rights outlined in the UNCRC.

In social work, broader human rights principles are also central to the profession. The International Federation of Social Workers provides a global definition of social work, which was approved in 2014 and is as follows:

> Social work is a practice-based profession and an academic discipline that promotes social change and development, social cohesion, and the empowerment and liberation of people. Principles of social justice, human rights, collective responsibility and respect for diversities are central to social work. Underpinned by theories of social work, social sciences, humanities and

indigenous knowledges, social work engages people and structures to address life challenges and enhance wellbeing. The above definition may be amplified at national and/or regional levels. (https://www.ifsw.org)

Furthermore, the profession is guided by the UN Sustainable Development Goals (SDGs), which contain a specific focus on shared decision making for all groups, particularly vulnerable groups, with the aim of creating 'responsive, inclusive, participatory, and representative decision-making at all levels' (SDG target 16.7).

With extensive and shared legal obligations in place that arise from being state signatories to the UNCRC (UN, 1989), it is a concern that young children under the age of 12 known to social services continue to lack opportunities to lay claim to their participation rights. Indeed, very young children still continue to be routinely left out and overlooked when it comes to decision making. They are not well informed, they do not know what plans are made on their behalf and, if they are involved, their experiences are often negative with their accounts not being listened to or considered (Alderson, 2008; Winter, 2010, 2010a, 2012; van Bijleveld et al, 2015; Balsells et al, 2017; Mateos et al, 2017; Husby et al, 2018, 2019; Diaz et al, 2018; Diaz, 2020; Juul and Husby, 2020; Falch Eriksen et al, 2021; Toros, 2021; Toros and Falch Eriksen, 2021; Mateos-Blanco et al, 2022; Salkauskiene et al, 2023; McCafferty and Mercado-Garcia, 2024). Because they experience ongoing exclusion and marginalisation, their participation rights and professionals' collaboration with them remains an aspiration rather than a reality (VOYPIC, 2013; Bouma et al, 2018; SAM, 2019; NICCY et al, 2022).

Exploring the contributory factors leading to the lack of progress regarding very young children's participation rights, specific research reveals that a combination of factors coalesces to disadvantage young children, including a tendency of professionals to underestimate the capacity and competencies of younger children, to avoid engaging in communicative encounters with young children because of a fear of making things worse or creating false expectations, and/or being unable to deal with their own emotional responses to children's distressing accounts (Winter, 2010a, 2011; van Bijleveld et al, 2015; Falch Eriksen et al, 2021; Toros, 2021; Salkauskiene et al, 2023; McCafferty and Mercado-Garcia, 2024). Furthermore, professionals believe that they lack the time, tools and training to effectively engage with younger children (Alderson, 2008; Winter, 2010a, 2011).

While a closer look at practice developments in local contexts reveals examples of very valuable practices in collaborating with young children (Guerreiro, 2022; Horgan and Kennan, 2021) these local pockets of good practice are not easily accessible in a transnational context. While there is also specific social work research that uses participatory approaches with very young children (aged eight and under) in the research process (Alderson, 2008; Winter, 2012; Winter et al, 2023), overall there is a dearth of similar social work research regarding young children, child welfare and their participation rights. Practice, research and policy development indicate that until now, efforts in relation to young children have been patchy and there is the ongoing exclusion of young children from decision-making fora. Professionals experience shared difficulties and barriers regarding its implementation. As a result, professionals are breaching their obligations under the UNCRC (Winter, 2011; Toros, 2021; Mateos-Blanco et al, 2022; McCafferty and Mercado-Garcia, 2024).

The aim of the PANDA project

Within the context just outlined, the focus of the PANDA project is on the participation rights of young children under the age of 12 years, in formal and informal child welfare-related decision-making processes and on developing collaboration between professionals and young children.

INTRODUCTION

The overarching aim of the project is to promote the participation rights of young children in decision-making processes and to help children find their voice in challenging times. The PANDA project does this through strengthening professionals' collaboration with young children involved in child welfare and child protection services by collating and disseminating learning materials for social workers, managers, policy officers and trainers.

Thus, we support the strengthening of the participation rights of young children at the policy level, at the organisational level, at the practitioner level and finally at the level of teachers, instructors and trainers.

The PANDA team

The project team together with the relevant associated partners (outlined in the following text), reflect the target groups of the project. We are convinced that in order to effectively realise a participatory mindset and participatory practice, this model of collaboration is the most meaningful. The project team therefore comprised eight partners from four countries – Belgium (Flanders), Northern Ireland, Norway and Spain – made up of universities, policy makers and field partners, as noted in Table 1.1.

Voice of Young People in Care (VOYPIC) is a nongovernmental organisation (NGO) based in Northern Ireland. It was created in 1993 by a group of young people in care and professionals, whose job is to promote the rights and voice of children in care and young people leaving care. Their aspiration is for every child in care to feel safe, valued and to be involved in decisions about their life. They provide a range of independent advocacy and participation services. They use their specialist knowledge and insight into the lives and experiences of children and young people, and work in partnership with them to influence legislation, policy and practice. The chief executive of VOYPIC is Alicia Tola.

Table 1.1: PANDA project members

Role	Name	Institution/agency
Project lead Project member	Wendy Eerdekens Eva Heirbaut	Artevelde University of Applied Sciences, Department of Social Work, Belgium (Flanders)
Regional coordinator Project member	Karen Winter Paul McCafferty	School of Social Sciences, Education and Social Work, Queen's University Belfast, Northern Ireland
Regional coordinator Project member	Inger-Sofie Husby Randi Juul	Norwegian University of Science and Technology, Trondheim, Norway
Regional coordinator Project members	Ester Mercado Garcia Maria Begoña Leyra Fatou Marta Blanco Carrasco Ana Isabel Corchado Castillo	Universidad Complutense de Madrid, Spain
Country agency lead Project member	Solvår Hernes Pål Børmark	Trondheim Kommune, Norway
Country agency lead Project members	Lisselotte Lowagie Linda Aerts Nele Haedens Virna Saenen	Opgroeien (Growing Up), a Flemish agency, Belgium.
Country agency lead Project member	Alicia Toal Geraldine McGuigan	Voice of Young People in Care (VOYPIC), Northern Ireland
Country agency lead Project member	Carmen Roncal Vargas Manuel Ortíz Mateos	Fundación Secretariado Gitano (FSG), Spain

INTRODUCTION

Fundación Secretariado Gitano (FSG) is a nonprofit intercultural social organisation that provides services to support the Roma community in Spain and Europe. Its activity began in the 1960s, but it was legally constituted in 1982. Its mission is to promote Roma access to rights, services, goods and social resources under the same conditions as other citizens.

During the process of the PANDA project, Professor Gillian Ruch from Sussex University was intensively involved. She was our critical friend, reflected with us, brought in new insights and reviewed the results.

The PANDA project also engaged associated partners who brought extensive expert knowledge and examples, presenting these during 'learning moments' (scheduled in the timetable of events), and they supported the dissemination process. The list of organisations is as follows: Ålesund and Fjord child protection services (Norway), Almediallas (Spain), Aspasi (Spain), Cachet vzw (Belgium), the Childcare Center from Madrid City Council (Spain), the Centre for Child Care and Family Support CKG Open Poortje (Belgium), the Dynamisation Service for Child and Adolescent Participation, Madrid City Council (Spain), One Family One Plan, Gezin Centraal (Belgium), the Health and Social Care Trusts (Northern Ireland), the Knowledge Centre for Children's Rights, Keki (Belgium), Flemish Office of the Children's Rights Commissioner (Belgium), Northern Ireland Association for the Care and Resettlement of Offenders (NIACRO) (Northern Ireland), the Office of Social Services (Northern Ireland), Proyecto Sirio (Spain) and REDidi (Spain).

The team represents people from different cultural backgrounds and with different expertise which we shared together. This placed us in an excellent position to build knowledge, approaches and methods from different perspectives and understandings. We believe that we have achieved better results by working in a transnational context.

We strived to help social workers so that they can collaborate with children, introducing new insights, methods and ideas in order to enable children to access their own voice and wider participation rights.

The objectives and target groups of the PANDA project

The project has four objectives:

- to create collaborative conditions for participatory social work with young children;
- to strengthen the competence of practitioners;
- to support the implementation of a participatory approach;
- to teach participatory tools by providing materials for trainers and educators.

In relation to professionals (including social workers, educators, psychologists, coaches, managers, policy makers, academics, trainers in the youth care, youth protection, education, early childhood and so on), the desired outcome is to increase the awareness of young children's participation rights and the benefits to children of their active participation in decisions about their own lives by providing knowledge of theoretical insights, conceptual frameworks, tools and approaches.

In relation to managers, the desired outcome is to increase knowledge of frameworks and guidelines that support the implementation of a participatory approach in their organisation, stimulate greater reflective practice, and support professionals to effectively translate child participation principles into practice.

In relation to policy makers, the desired outcome is that they have access to practical, user-friendly and applied frameworks and guidelines which they can adopt as templates to inform the delivery of services.

In relation to trainers, the desire outcome is that they have more knowledge of the law, theory and methods, approaches and practices to underpin training and skills development.

The achievements of the PANDA Project

A website (https://reacch.eu) with texts, presentations, podcasts and vimeos in English, Dutch, Norwegian and Spanish hosts the achievements of the PANDA project. Its construction reflects the development and consolidation of our participatory learning process over three years, which was premised on close cooperation between the eight project partners and guided by the needs of the different target groups. Reflecting participatory processes, our own outputs were designed as part of an iterative process where ideas were explored, developed and adjusted over time.

The acronym of the REACCH website stands for Resources for Engaging and Collaborating with Children. It hosts several pages with the main content, which are as follows.

The *media library* contains four briefs outlining: (a) theoretical and conceptual frameworks on the subject of participation of young children; (b) the methods and tools for engaging with young children; (c) crucial communication processes and skill for a participatory approach; and (d) challenges and opportunities for participation with young children. There are also testimonials from professionals.

Policy and management guidelines contain opportunities for reflection, review and refreshing approaches where possible. We learned during the process that the initial idea of designing a framework was not workable because legal, policy and management frameworks that already exist in different countries vary considerably. We agreed that guidelines provided a better way of supporting organisations to review their current policies, procedures and to implement a participatory policy and support its continued use. The guidelines offer tools to determine a vision, objectives and a way of working within each specific context. There is a 'brief' or summary document explaining the legal framework of the UNCRC and this is accompanied by four other briefs on child welfare and child protection legislation in the participating countries involved in the project. There are also testimonials on the implementation of a participatory approach and participatory frameworks.

A toolkit for trainers is also available to support the training of social professionals in realising a participatory approach. There is a manual and four sets of exercises on law, challenges and opportunities, group participation, tools, and methods. The purpose of the toolkit is to provide guidance, exercises, structured sessions and reflective space for trainers who train professionals.

Shared PANDA principles and young children's participation rights

The PANDA project reflects a process of learning, searching, adjusting and of occasionally losing our way and of not knowing. Through deepening our dialogue with each other, certain crucial elements regarding children's participation rights gradually emerged. These are shared in common and create a common collective understanding.

The project began shortly before the COVID-19 pandemic and had to adapt plans with a year of intensive online meetings rather than face-to-face encounters. The online meetings continued throughout the three years, although less frequently. We were relieved that in years two and three of the project, a face-to-face learning week could take place in Ghent, Trondheim and Belfast. Each country team also had learning sessions with a wider group of professionals in their own region. We were also able to conclude with a closing meeting in Madrid. In this way, our learning community around this theme was strengthened and consolidated.

We learned a lot and emerged enriched from the process. Our experiences have enabled us to highlight a number of issues that may be recognisable to a wider audience when it comes to the participation of young children in child welfare and child protection, and the transnational exchange about this.

What's in a name?

The UNCRC talks about participation rights. However, this has become a catch-all concept that has several layers. Everyone is looking for other concepts that better express what this is. In Norway, people talk about collaboration, while in Flanders, they talk about partnership. What do we mean by that? Will we find a concept that fully reflects what we mean?

It's about the mindset

Learning how to work in participatory ways is not about demonstrating learning in a technical way. It stems from and requires a particular mindset underpinned by the values of respect for the human worth, value and dignity of each individual regardless of their age, ethnicity, language, religion, disability, sexuality, geography, nationality or culture. Valuing participatory processes means accepting that you never reach the finish line as the process is iterative. We therefore speak of a participatory attitude.

It's a process

It is not just about participating every now and then. Participation is relational, part of everyday life and everyone's responsibility. We say this because if we look at concrete practices, we see great examples of participation with young children. However, it is still too often seen as the responsibility of certain people or certain organisations that are perceived to be 'good at it'. Moreover, practices are still rarely exposed and shared. We wish to stress that participatory practice is the responsibility of *all* people who work with young children.

The importance of context

The way we all work with young children cannot simply be copied from one context to another. The local history and cultural context has an impact on the daily practice. Transnational exchange and learning about Roma families and about the Troubles in Northern Ireland made this clearer. It especially helps to see what we can do to act and develop policies that are more in line with the context in which our families live.

The importance of reflecting and dialogue

In the PANDA project we mainly learned from talking with each other and reflecting on how we think about the participation of young children. We wish to emphasise the importance of reflective, safe spaces where the development of a curious and inquisitive mind can be encouraged and where we can look to each other for words to express ourselves so that the other person understands better what is meant. Reflective spaces helped us challenge and adjust our own ideas, assumptions, biases and perspectives, and encouraged us to develop our own participatory mindset and attitude in order to facilitate young children to access their full place as subjects in their lives and in society:

> It made me aware that *when* participation starts is a crucial feature i.e. does participation only start once you're meeting a child and their family or is there something that starts before that in terms of a mindset and the wider policy agenda that determines the frame of reference practitioners meeting children have in mind. There's something important about this interface between the different contextual levels that it's vital that participation and a commitment to it is reflected in policy and legislation but that also participation is understood as a mindset that practitioners need to be developing. It's a strong reminder that working in participatory ways

requires a constant and dynamic dialogue that involves thinking, feeling and action. (Ruch, 2021)

We hope that this handbook will support you in working participatively with young children in youth care, youth protection and beyond, and that it also encourages you to reflect, communicate and collaborate on the central tenets of participatory approaches and practices.

References

Alderson, P. (2008) *Young Children's Rights: Exploring Beliefs, Attitudes, Principles and Practice*, London: Jessica Kingsley.

Balsells, M.Á., Fuentes-Peláez, N. and Pastor, C. (2017) 'Listening to the voices of children in decision-making: A challenge for the child protection system in Spain', *Children and Youth Services Review*, 79: 418–425.

Bouma, H., López, M.L., Knorth, E.J. and Grietens, H. (2018) 'Meaningful participation for children in the Dutch child protection system: A critical analysis of relevant provisions in policy documents', *Child Abuse and Neglect*, 79: 279–292.

Diaz, C. (2020) *Decision Making in Child and Family Social Work: Perspectives on Children's Participation*, Bristol: Policy Press.

Diaz, C., Pert, H. and Thomas, N. (2018) ' "Just another person in the room": Young people's views on their participation in child in care reviews', *Adoption & Fostering*, 42(4): 369–382.

Falch-Eriksen, A. and Toros, K. (2021) *Professional Practice in Child Protection and the Child's Right to Participate*, Abingdon: Routledge.

Falch-Eriksen, A., Toros, K., Sindi, I. and Lehtme, R. (2021) 'Children expressing their views in child protection casework: Current research and their rights going forward', *Child and Family Social Work*, 26(3): 485–497.

Guerreiro, A.I. (2022) *Children's Rights in Health Care Practice: A Guide for Doctors, Nurses, and Other Health Care Professionals*, Abingdon: Routledge.

Horgan, D. and Kennan, D. (eds) (2021) *Child and Youth Participation in Policy, Practice and Research*, Abingdon: Routledge.

Husby, I.S.D., Kiik, R. and Juul, R. (2019) 'Children's encounters with professionals: Recognition and respect during collaboration', *European Journal of Social Work*, 22(6): 987–998.

Husby, I.S.D., Slettebø, T. and Juul, R. (2018) 'Partnerships with children in child welfare: The importance of trust and pedagogical support', *Child & Family Social Work*, 23(3): 443–450.

Juul, R. and Husby, I.S.D. (2020) 'Collaboration and conversations with children in child welfare services: Parents' viewpoint', *Child & Family Social Work*, 25: 9–17.

Mateos-Blanco, T., Sánchez-Lissen, E., Gil-Jaurena, I. and Romero-Pérez, C. (2022) 'Child-led participation: A scoping review of empirical studies', *Social Inclusion*, 10(2): 32–42.

Mateos, A., Vaquero, E., Balsells, M.À. and Ponce, C. (2017) '"They didn't tell me anything; they just sent me home": Children's participation in the return home', *Child and Family Social Work*, 22(2): 871–880.

McCafferty, P. and Mercado Garcia, E. (2024) 'Children's participation in child welfare: a systematic review of systematic reviews', *British Journal of Social Work*, 54(3): 1092–1108.

Northern Ireland Commissioner for Children and Young People, Children and Young People's Commissioner Scotland, Children's Commissioner for Wales (2022) *Report of the Children's Commissioners of Northern Ireland, Scotland and Wales to the United Nations Committee on the Rights of the Child. Examination of the Combined Sixth and Seventh Periodic Reports of the United Kingdom of Great Britain and Northern Ireland*, Belfast: NICCY.

Ruch, G. (2021). *The Panda Project. Internal Progress Review, November 2021* (internal report). Resources for Engaging and Collaborating with Children (REACCH). https://reacch.eu/nl/home-nl/

Salkauskiene, I., Wilson, S., Gresdahl, M. and Juul, R. (2023) 'Children's experiences of collaborative relationship with child welfare and protection professionals in Norway: A state-of-the-art review', *Nordic Social Work Research*, 1–17.

SAM (SAM Steunpunt Mense n Samenleving) (2019) *Sociaal Werk in Transitie*. Aanbevelingen voor het Vlaamse en federale beleid. Brussels, Belgium: SAM Steunpunt Mense n Samenleving.

Toal, A. (2022). *A Voice for Children*. [vimeo]. https://vimeo.com/835685935

Toros, K. (2021) 'A systematic review of children's participation in child protection decision-making: Tokenistic presence or not?', *Children and Society*, 35(3): 395–411.

Toros, K. and Falch-Eriksen, A. (2021) '"I do not want to cause additional pain": Child protection workers' perspectives on child participation in child protection practice', *Journal of Family Social Work*, 24(1): 43–59.

United Nations (1989) *Convention on the Rights of the Child*, Geneva: United Nations.

Van Bijleveld, G.G., Dedding, C.W. and Bunders-Aelen, J.F. (2015) 'Children's and young people's participation within child welfare and child protection services: A state-of-the-art review', *Child and Family Social Work*, 20(2): 129–138.

VOYPIC (Voice of Young People in Care) (2013) *Our Life in Care*. VOYPIC's Third CASI Survey of the Views and Experiences of Children and Young People in Care. Belfast, Northern Ireland: VOYPIC.

Winter, K. (2010a) *Building Relationships and Communicating with Young Children: A Practical Guide for Social Workers*, Abingdon: Routledge.

Winter, K. (2010b) 'The perspectives of young children in care about their circumstances and implications for social work practice', *Child and Family Social Work*, 15(2): 186–195.

Winter, K. (2011) 'The UNCRC and social workers' relationships with young children', *Child Abuse Review*, 20(6): 395–406.

Winter, K. (2012) 'Ascertaining the perspectives of young children in care: Case studies in the use of reality boxes', *Children and Society*, 26(5): 368–380.

Winter, K., Sebba, J., Tah, P., Connolly, P., Roberts, J. and Millen, S. (2023) 'Using the talking album to elicit the views of young children in foster care regarding a reading intervention', *Qualitative Social Work*, 22(6): 1175–1190.

TWO

Young children's rights

Karen Winter

Introduction

In Chapter 1, the context to the PANDA project was set out. A fundamental commitment to the participation rights of babies, infants and very young children, and the implementation of these rights in practice is the driving force in the project. While we all share the same legal obligations as state signatories to the United Nations Convention on the Rights of the Child (UNCRC), we are aware that, first, professional knowledge about children's rights can sometimes be patchy and underdeveloped, and second, that very young children are often overlooked in relation to their participation rights. In this chapter, we explore what children's rights are, what the UNCRC has to say about very young children's participation rights, and why these are central to social work practice in the area of child welfare and child protection.

The United Nations Convention on the Rights of the Child

As professionals working with children in child welfare and child protection, we all share moral, social and legal obligations to respect the worth of each individual child and their views, perspectives and experiences, irrespective of their characteristics. These legal obligations are outlined in the UNCRC and the supporting General Comments, published by the Committee on the Rights of the Child, which give detailed guidance on implementation of specific rights outlined in the UNCRC.

The UNCRC (UN, 1989) defines individual children's civil, cultural, economic, social and political rights, noting that all children have these rights regardless of their characteristics (for example, their age, religion, disability, sexuality, or their cultural, religious and linguistic background). The rights set out in the UNCRC comprise 54 articles which are indivisible, interrelated, contingent and contextual.

Loosely categorised as protection, provision and participation rights (Alderson, 2008), the PANDA project has primarily been concerned with young children's participation rights (that is, every child's right to express their views freely on any matter relating to them and the provision of the opportunity to be heard). The UNCRC ensures that children's participation rights are promoted in practice through the provisions contained in the four underlying principles (Articles 2, 3, 6 and 12). These four foundational principles are depicted in Figure 2.1 and are explained further in the following discussion.

Article 2 notes our obligation to respect and ensure the rights set out in the Convention without discrimination, irrespective of the child and/or their parents/legal guardians' race, colour, sex, language, religion, political or other opinion, national, ethnic or social origin, property, disability, birth or other status.

Article 3 notes that in all actions concerning children (whether undertaken by public or social welfare private social welfare institutions), the best interests of the child shall be the primary consideration.

Article 6 recognises that every child has the inherent right to life and our obligation to ensure, to the maximum extent possible, the survival and development of the child.

Figure 2.1: The four foundational pillars of the UNCRC

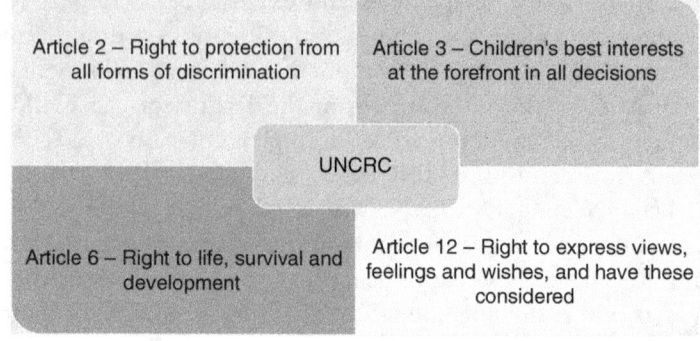

Article 12 notes our obligation to assure to the child who is capable of forming their own views the right to express those views freely in all matters affecting the child, the views being due weight in accordance with the age and maturity of the child. In particular, there is an obligation to provide the child with the opportunity to be heard in judicial and administrative proceedings affecting them, either directly or indirectly through a representative or appropriate body.

Several other articles of the UNCRC are also relevant regarding children's participation rights and, as depicted in Figure 2.2, these include Articles 5, 13, 14, 15 and 17.

Article 5 notes that the responsibilities and duties of parents, legal guardians to provide direction and support to children in the exercise of their rights in line with their evolving capacities should be respected.

Article 13 recognises the right of children to freedom of expression and that they have the right to seek, receive, impart information and ideas of all kinds orally, in writing, print, art or through any other media of the child's choice.

Article 14 outlines the obligation to respect a child's right to freedom of thought, conscience and religion, and Article 15 contains the right to freedom of association and peaceful assembly.

Figure 2.2: The interrelated UNCRC articles that define children's participation rights

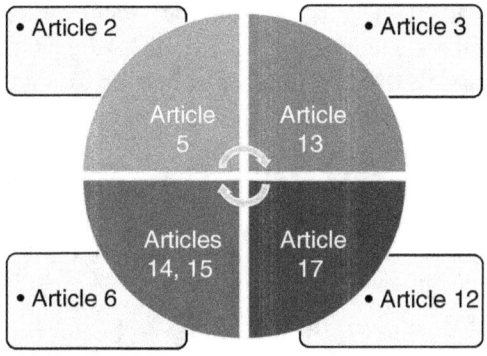

Article 17 recognises the role played by mass media in children's lives and outlines their right of access to information from a range of national and international sources, especially information aimed at promoting their overall wellbeing.

Some of the most influential work on conceptualising the contextual aspects of the implementation of the Article 12 right is published by Professor Laura Lundy, whose own model has been implemented in legal, policy and practice frameworks across the world. Lundy (2007) provides an outline of the original model, and Kennan et al (2019) and Ward and Lundy (2024) highlight its translation into child welfare and early childhood practice.

The General Comments

Recognising the complexities and challenges of implementing children's rights, the Committee on the Rights of the Child has published a series of General Comments. The General Comments, published by the Committee on the Rights of the Child (CRC), are official documents and are the UN's detailed interpretation of an article of the UNCRC, specifically focused not just on interpreting it in detail, but also giving guidance and advice on the practicalities of implementation. A full list of all the General Comments is available on the website of the United Nations Office of the High Commissioner, Human Rights (https://www.ohchr.org/en/treaty-bodies/crc/general-comments).

As explored by Lundy (2019) and of particular relevance to the participation rights of young children are the following:

- General Comment No. 7: Implementing Child Rights in Early Childhood (CRC, 2005)
- General Comment No. 9: The Rights of Children with Disabilities (CRC, 2006)
- General Comment No. 12: The Right of the Child to Be Heard (CRC, 2009)
- General Comment No. 14: The Right of the Child to Have Their Best Interests Taken as the Primary Consideration (CRC, 2013)

Applying children's rights in child welfare/child protection

In the spheres of child welfare and child protection, most social workers have heard of Article 12 and know this as children's participation rights. However, as was illustrated earlier, all rights in the UNCRC are interrelated and indivisible. This means that Article 12 cannot be considered in isolation from other relevant articles. Hence, if we again consider a child's right to express their views and have those considered under Article 12, we also need to think about Article 2 (nondiscrimination – all children regardless of their age have a right to express views and have these considered), Article 3 (what is in the best interests of the child), Article 5 (the evolving capacities of the child) and Articles 13 and 17 (the right to receive and impart information. Children have a right to receive accessible information about the issues and the implications as part of their Article 12 rights. The best way of illustrating what this all means in practice is further considering the various articles and their implementation in relation to very young children.

Beginning with Article 12, it does not specifically include the words 'participation rights' and, as articulated by Lundy (2007), the wording of Article 12 is more complicated than is often acknowledged. It refers to terms such as (a) capable, (b) expressing views freely, (c) opportunity to be heard, and (d) views being given due weight. For professionals working in child protection and child welfare, there are common questions that need to be addressed, and the chapter attempts to do this in what follows.

Does a very young child have capacity and agency?

In our work with children, professionals often slip into thinking and assuming that a very young child is not capable because they do not have a fully formed vocabulary to put together whole sentences, for example. This is a narrow approach to understanding children's participation rights and overlooks the fact that very young children communicate in a myriad of intricate, highly nuanced, nonverbal and preverbal always other than fully formed sentences. It is incumbent on adults to adapt, accept and engage with these myriad of ways of communicating rather than discriminating against the very youngest children by not respecting them as individuals with a contribution to make and not respecting the multiple and varied ways in which they communicate.

Article 2 UNCRC provides the legal basis to this in outlining a child's right to be protected from all forms of discrimination, including discrimination on the basis of age. General Comment No. 7 (CRC, 2005, para 14: 6–7), which provides detailed guidance on the implementation of children's rights in early childhood, illustrates this further when it states that:

> Respect for the young child's agency – as a participant in family, community and society – is frequently

overlooked, or rejected as inappropriate on the grounds of age and immaturity. In many countries and regions, traditional beliefs have emphasised young children's need for training and socialisation. They have been regarded as undeveloped, lacking even basic capacities for understanding, communicating and making choices. They have been powerless within their families, and often voiceless and invisible within society. The Committee wishes to emphasise that article 12 applies both to younger and to older children. As holders of rights, even the youngest children are entitled to express their views, which should be 'given due weight in accordance with the age and maturity of the child'.

Reinforcing the obligations on adults, General Comment No. 7 (CRC, 2005, para 14(c): 7) says that that the obligation is on 'adults to adopt a child-centred attitude, listening to young children and respecting their dignity and their individual points of view. It also requires adults to show patience and creativity by adapting their expectations to a young child's interests, levels of understanding and preferred ways of communicating'. These approaches show regard and respect for children's evolving capacities, as explored in detail in work by Lansdown (2005).

How can social workers respect very young children's agency?

It is one thing to say that we must respect very young children's agency and another to fully understand what this means and how we go about doing this in practice. There are two conceptual frameworks that can help here.

The first is that when the UNCRC was being drafted, the sociology of childhood was also emerging as a new way of thinking about children and childhood. The sociology of childhood (James and Prout, 2003; Cosaro and Everitt, 2024) proposes that rather than viewing very young children as immature and incapable of making valid contributions to their relationships and surroundings, such children do have the capacity to make valid contributions to decisions about their lives and can, if given the opportunity to do so, exercise varying degrees of power and influence. For example, if a child resists carers' attempts to encourage them to put their shoes on or wash their hands, they are expressing their agency. If a child has a temper tantrum because someone has said 'no' to something, they are expressing their agency.

Therefore, the second conceptual framework that helps practitioners is to accept that in apparently small interactions between children and adults, children can express their agency. It also means accepting that often the barrier to these expressions of agency having meaning, power and influence in decision making is not with the young children, but rather with the adults who give no significance or weight to the child's expressed views.

Accepting that children have agency is simply accepting that all children can express their views. However, it is also important to note that the concept of agency is complicated, in that a child's expression of their agency is not absolute – that is, they are not always afforded the opportunity to follow through on expressions of agentic capacity, but rather agentic capacity is a negotiated, relational and dynamic process between child and parent/carer, where other issues – such as what is in the best interests of the child and what are the protection rights of the child – also need to be considered. In coming to decisions where children have expressed their agentic capacity, the respectful approach that adults should adopt is to explain the rationale behind the decisions made.

How do we assess if a very young child has capacity and agency?

Professionals often fall into the trap of deeming a child not capable simply by virtue of their age and developmental status. However, the UNCRC and the General Comments challenge this mindset, indicating that a positive, affirming and enabling attitude towards young children and their capacity is required. For example, on the concept of capable of forming views, General Comment No. 12 (CRC, 2009, paras 20 and 21: 9) states that:

> This phrase should not be seen as a limitation, but rather as an obligation for States parties to assess the capacity of the child to form an autonomous opinion to the greatest extent possible. This means that States parties cannot begin with the assumption that a child is incapable of expressing her or his own views. On the contrary, States parties should presume that a child has the capacity to form her or his own views and recognise that she or he has the right to express them; it is not up to the child to first prove her or his capacity. The Committee emphasises that article 12 imposes no age limit on the right of the child to express her or his views and discourages States parties from introducing age limits either in law or in practice which would restrict the child's right to be heard in all matters affecting her or him.

The same General Comment also notes (CRC, 2009, para 29: 11) that:

> By requiring that due weight be given in accordance with age and maturity, article 12 makes it clear that age alone cannot determine the significance of a child's views. Children's levels of understanding are not uniformly linked to their biological age. Research has shown that information, experience, environment, social and cultural expectations, and levels of support all contribute to the development of a child's capacities to form a view. For this reason, the views of the child have to be assessed on a case-by-case examination.

This requires professionals to avoid assumptions about children's age-related abilities and capacities. This can be challenging when assessment frameworks and practice tools can rely on a rather crude and age-related model of child development.

How do we recognise a very young child's right to express their own views freely?

If we do not believe that a child is capable, it is easy to overlook and trivialise the ways in which they can and do communicate. General Comment No. 7 (CRC, 2005, para 14: 7) challenges our mistaken assumptions when it states that:

> As holders of rights, even the youngest children are entitled to express their views, which should be 'given due weight in accordance with the age and maturity of the child' (art. 12.1). Young children are acutely sensitive to their surroundings and very rapidly acquire understanding of the people, places and routines in their lives, along with awareness of their own unique identity. They make choices and communicate their feelings, ideas and wishes in numerous ways, long before they are able to communicate through the conventions of spoken or written language.

Following on from this, the same General Comment (CRC, 2005, para 14c: 7) notes the obligation to ensure that parents and professionals 'take all appropriate measures to promote the active involvement of parents, professionals and responsible authorities in the creation of opportunities for young children to progressively exercise their rights within their everyday activities in all relevant settings, including by providing training in the necessary skills'.

In practice, as outlined in General Comment No. 12 (CRC, 2009, para 21: 9) what this means is that there is recognition of and respect for the following:

(a) Nonverbal forms of communication including play, body language, facial expressions, and drawing

and painting, through which very young children demonstrate understanding, choices and preferences.
(b) It is not necessary that the child has comprehensive knowledge of all aspects of the matter affecting them, but that they have sufficient understanding to be capable of appropriately forming their own views on the matter.
(c) The varied ways in which children communicate – for example, 'children with disabilities should be equipped with, and enabled to use, any mode of communication necessary to facilitate the expression of their views. Efforts must also be made to recognise the right to expression of views for minority, indigenous and migrant children and other children who do not speak the majority language'.
(d) The need to develop sensitive, attuned, child-focused and considerate practice to avoid the negative consequences for a child of the inconsiderate practice of this right.
(e) The need to supply accessible, meaningful information adapted to children's preferences to inform them on what issues their views are being sought. This is adapted depending on the skills, interests of children in line with their evolving capacities (Lansdown, 2005) as explored further below.

These practice principles also include providing accessible, meaningful information about the reasons why children's views are being sought, how their views will be considered, how children will be informed about the ways in which their views were considered, and what impact children's views had on decisions made, as noted in Article 5 UNCRC, which states that:

> States Parties shall respect the responsibilities, rights and duties of parents or, where applicable, the members of the extended family or community as provided for by

local custom, legal guardians or other persons legally responsible for the child, to provide, in a manner consistent with the evolving capacities of the child, appropriate direction and guidance in the exercise by the child of the rights recognised in the present Convention.

What does it mean to give 'due weight' to a young child's views and how do we do this?

Let's assume that you have managed to ascertain a young child's views, feelings and experiences using methods and approaches reflective of their preferences and choices, and that you have ensured that the views, experiences and feelings are fully represented in decision-making processes. You will be aware that there is a process of adults/decision makers giving due weight to a child's views. In practice, 'giving something due weight' refers to how much importance and significance is attached (in this case) to the child's expressed views. Factors that are often relevant in such considerations include the following:

- *Child factors*: how old is the child, what developmental needs do they have, how far do they comprehend the issues at stake and the implications of different options in decision making, how capable are they of forming a view and so on.
- *Parent/carer factors*: are the parents/carers supportive or opposed to different options in decision making, do the parents have the capacity and supports they need dependent on the option chosen and so on.
- *Contextual factors*: the seriousness of the issue, the presence of any threats, abuse, intimidation, violence or coercion, the cultural, social, economic, religious, ethnic and political context, and the short- and long-term impacts and implications of particular decisions.

Sometimes, there can be a tendency not to attribute significance or importance to an expressed view because it is not verbally stated in an articulate way. A young child's view can be overlooked as insignificant and/or unimportant. And yet, as indicated in the UNCRC and the supporting General Comments, a child's expressed views, feelings and experiences through play acting, drawing, singing, making things, temper tantrums, withdrawing, silence, shouting, screaming, playing, kicking, colouring, mimicking, eye movements, gestures, and jumping up and down can all convey so much, and we are obliged to adapt our own attitude and approach to be attuned to this.

How do we reconcile young children's views and what is deemed to be in their best interests?

Another reason that a child's view is not attributed significance or importance is because professionals often come across situations where the child's views (Article 12) are not aligned to what adults have decided is in their best interests (Article 3). In such situations, it is easy for professionals to dismiss a young child's view as uninformed, partial or inaccurate. This is wrong and reflects a fundamental misunderstanding about Articles 3 and 12. Many professionals see these as two contradictory and opposing rights, but General Comment No. 12 (CRC, 2009, para 74: 18) reminds us that:

> There is no tension between articles 3 and 12, only a complementary role of the two general principles: one establishes the objective of achieving the best interests of the child and the other provides the methodology for reaching the goal of hearing either the child or the children. In fact, there can be no correct application of article 3 if the components of article 12 are not respected. Likewise, article 3 reinforces the functionality of article 12, facilitating the essential role of children in all decisions affecting their lives.

It is noteworthy that in implementing Article 3, the best interests of the child can only be served by ensuring that every child has the opportunity to express their views freely and that these are considered. This means that in all instances, the adults are obliged to consider the views of child, but they must also come to a decision which is in the best interests of the child, where a child might not be happy with the outcome, but where the explanation is reasonable considering the best interests and the wider protection and provision rights of the child.

How do we create opportunities for very young children to express their views freely and ensure their views are considered?

Table 2.1 outlines key best practice principles for working with children and promoting their participation. In the subsequent chapters, we will explore ways in which opportunities are created for very young children to express their views. The creation of opportunities relies on interrelated values on our parts, namely:

- An attitude and mindset that starts from the premise that all children can express their views.
- A belief that the myriad of ways in which children express their views are all equally valid.
- A commitment to sharing children's views, feelings and experiences in a way that ensures that these are given the same consideration as the views of the adults involved.
- A commitment to showing how and in what ways children's views have been considered, and how and in what ways they have had an influence.
- A commitment to informing children about the influence and impact of their views on decision making.

In terms of practicalities, we need to ensure the following:

- The provision of relevant, accessible information to children about why their views are being sought.

Table 2.1: Best practice principles in working with children

Practice principles	Meaning
Transparent and informative	Children must be provided with full, accessible, diversity-sensitive and age-appropriate information about their right to express their views freely, the weight to be given to their views and how this participation will take place, its scope, purpose and potential impact.
Voluntary	Children should never be coerced into expressing views against their wishes and they should be informed that they can cease involvement at any stage.
Respectful	Children's views have to be treated with respect. Adults should create opportunities, understand the social and economic context of children's lives, and build on good practice.
Relevant	Issues should be of relevance to the children, selected by themselves and allow for children to draw on their knowledge, skills and abilities.
Child-friendly	Environments and methods should be adapted to children's capacities. Adequate time, resources, preparation and support should be made available and sensitive to different cultural backgrounds.
Inclusive	Participation should be non-discriminatory and encouraging to marginalised groups of children.
Supported by training	Adults need preparation, skills and support to facilitate children's participation effectively. Adults should be provided with skills in listening, working jointly with children and engaging them effectively in accordance with their evolving capacities.
Safe and sensitive to risk	Adults need to be aware of and minimise the risks posed to some children by virtue of their involvement in decision making.
Accountable	Children must be informed as to how their views have been interpreted and used, and how their views have influenced any outcomes. Monitoring and evaluation of children's participation needs to be undertaken, where possible, with children themselves.

Source: Adapted from General Comment No. 12 (CRC, 2009, para 134: 29–30)

- The creation of safe, familiar, friendly and supportive spaces to share views.
- The provision of child-friendly approaches reflecting children's own choices and preferences.

General Comment No. 12 also outlines the principles that must underpin all processes in which a child (or children) is heard and/or participates.

In the following chapters, we will be considering the application of these principles in in professional practice in child welfare contexts, with examples of children's participation rights drawn from European countries involved in the PANDA project. The principles are shared across contexts, and yet practice and approaches vary. This reflects the different social, economic, cultural contexts of the different countries and, within this, their differing legal frameworks. The differing country contexts and legal frameworks that govern child welfare are outlined in Chapter 3, before the subsequent chapters move on to consider various practice examples.

References

Alderson, P. (2008) *Young Children's Rights: Exploring Beliefs, Principles and Practice*, London: Jessica Kingsley.

CRC (Committee on the Rights of the Child) (2005) *General Comment No. 7: Implementing Child Rights in Early Childhood*, Geneva: United Nations.

CRC (2006) *General Comment No. 9: The Rights of Children with Disabilities*, Geneva: United Nations.

CRC (2009) *General Comment No. 12: The Right of the Child to Be Heard*, Geneva: United Nations.

CRC (2013) *General Comment No. 14: The Right of the Child to Have Their Best Interests Taken as the Primary Consideration*, Geneva: United Nations.

Cosaro, W.A. and Everitt, J.D. (2024) *The Sociology of Childhood*, Thousand Oaks, CA: Sage.

James, A. and Prout, A. (2003) *Constructing and Reconstructing Childhood: Contemporary Issues in the Sociological Study of Childhood*, London: Routledge.

Kennan, D., Brady, B. and Forkan, C. (2019) 'Space, voice, audience and influence: The Lundy model of participation (2007) in child welfare practice', *Practice*, 31(3): 205–218.

Lansdown, G. (2005) *The Evolving Capacities of Children: Implications for the Exercise of Rights*, Florence: UNICEF Innocenti Research Centre.

Lundy, L. (2007) '"Voice' is not enough": Conceptualising Article 12 of the United Nations Convention on the Rights of the Child', *British Educational Research Journal*, 33(6): 927–942.

Lundy, L. (2019) 'Implementing the rights of young children: An assessment of the impact of General Comment no. 7 on Law and Policy on a Global Scale', in J. Murray, B. Blue Swadener and K. Smith (eds) *The Routledge Handbook of Young Children's Rights*, Abingdon: Routledge, pp 15–28.

United Nations (1989) *Convention on the Rights of the Child*, Geneva: United Nations.

Ward, C. and Lundy, L. (2024) 'Space, voice, audience, and influence: The Lundy model and early childhood', in L. Mahony et al (eds) *Early Childhood Voices: Children, Families, Professionals*, Cham: Springer International, pp 17–28.

THREE

Contextual influences on participation

Wendy Eerdekens, Eva Heirbaut, Karen Winter, Alicia Toal,
Geraldine McGuigan, Carmen Roncal Vargas, Manuel Ortíz Mateos,
Inger Sofie Dahlø Husby and Randi Juul

Introduction

The last chapter set out our shared legal obligations under the United Nations Convention on the Rights of the Child (UNCRC) (UN, 1989) in relation to the participation rights of young children. While the countries involved in the PANDA project (and indeed all countries that are state signatories to the UNCRC) have these shared legal obligations under the UNCRC, each country has a different social, economic, political and cultural context, and these contextual differences are also reflected in the different legal frameworks concerning child welfare. In this chapter, we briefly outline the differing legal frameworks governing child welfare in Belgium, Spain, Northern Ireland and Norway. The aim of the chapter is to highlight the significance of context when thinking about the policy and practice of very young children's participation rights.

Introduction to the country context: Flanders (Belgium)

Belgium is a small country with about 11.7 million inhabitants, but has a complex state structure. It is a federal state, divided into three communities and three regions. The communities are based on the official languages: German (East), French (Wallonia, South) and Dutch (Flanders, North). These communities have authority over several domains which provide support for people in need (Eerdekens et al, 2022).

Positioning of child welfare services within the Belgian policy structure

Due to the complex state structure, social services for children, young people and families in Belgium involve many agencies and facilities. Moreover, responsibilities are divided among various levels of government. For example, residential care and youth justice are federal and thus regulated for the entire country, whereas outpatient mental health care is regulated at the community level (Eerdekens et al, 2022).

Integral youth care

Child welfare policies have evolved over time, reflecting changing discourses and issues of concern in the wider society. While the emphasis used to be on child protection, more recently, increasing attention has been paid to children's participation rights and the contexts in which those rights are supported. The ratification of the United Nations Convention on the Rights of the Child (UNCRC) (UN, 1989) by Belgium in 1992 provided significant momentum for this change. Since 2013, child welfare has been regulated by the Decree on Integral Youth Care (Eerdekens et al, 2022). This decree has six principles. The first principle is known as 'the socialisation of youth care'. This means that services, in developing their response to families, should ensure that the social context and the social networks of families are considered in all policies, practices and plans to support children and their parents/carers. Services should also be premised on strength-based approaches to families and they should be designed in ways that empower and enable children and parents/carers to fully participate in society.

Building on this, the second principle is 'early access to child welfare when necessary' and these services must be useful, accessible, available, comprehensible, affordable, underpinned by transparent policies and be delivered in collaboration with other similar services. This joined-up approach based on a low-threshold, directly accessible model of service delivery is crucial. A third related principle relates to the availability of 'crisis child welfare services' which must be available, so that when there is an acute crisis, there is a quick and appropriate response. The current crisis programme comprises four fixed elements: contact point (hotline), short-term intervention of a few days in the context of the child, crisis coaching and supervision, and crisis residential care.

With regard to the delivery of care, the fourth principle is that it is based on 'guaranteed continuity' of relationship and service where possible. Related to this, the fifth principle is that professionals delivering the services must be equipped and ready in 'dealing with situations of risk'. Every professional is responsible and must be able to deal with problematic family situations, discussing their concerns directly with families and by working together to explore options as to how the situation can be improved. If this is not sufficient, professionals can refer to or be supported by two specialised services (both of which can refer to and seek intervention by the courts). Lastly, the sixth principle is 'participation'. This is important on three levels: individual cases, level of the services, and the structural policy level.

Children's participation supported by a decree

Since 2006, the decree on the legal position of minors in child welfare has guaranteed their participation and fundamental rights (DRM, 2019). The decree was amended in 2019. It states that every minor is capable of exercising their rights independently, without an age limit. For some rights, the minor must be competent. This includes the right to consent to the assistance offered, the right to access their file and the right not to be separated from their parents against their will. It is assumed that a minor from the age of 12 is competent, but any caregiver can also assess a child under 12 as competent (Vlaanderen, 2024).

Several articles in this decree specifically address participation as follows. First, there is reference to 'informed consent' (in which children deemed competent must consent and be informed about the consequences of refusing assistance). Second, there is reference to the 'provision of accessible information' (including information about the diagnosis, duration of assistance and complaint procedures). Third, 'children's participation in decision making' is embedded throughout. The approach to participation is founded on the principles outlined in the UNCRC (see Chapter 2). As such, children are positioned as partners. The consequence of this is that where a social worker disagrees with a child, for example, this must be documented in the file. Fourth, 'children's right to a file' is noted. Related to this, every child has the right to a carefully maintained file. A framework has been developed for access and for parents' opposition to certain parts of the file. A competent child also has access to their file. Lastly, in supporting children to exercise their rights, 'children have the right to a confidant who supports them' in exercising their rights. This person should not be involved in the care process.

Young children's participation in practice

The 'Growing Up' agency is an entity of the Flemish Ministry of Welfare, Public Health and Family, and is responsible for implementing the decrees. It supports participative child welfare and protection in the following ways. First, within their own community services, Signs of Safety (a strengths-based approach to child protection work, see Turnell and Edwards, 1997) has been implemented since 2016. This approach (or elements of it) are also applied in other organisations. Second, organisations invite collaborative relationships with service users by invitations to monthly meetings, for example, to share their ideas on how participation can be better operationalised in practice. Third, each organisation has a procedure for complaints. And fourth, there are several organisations for individuals with experience in child welfare. Two of them are subsidised by the 'Growing Up' agency: Cachet vzw for youngsters and Ouderspunt for parents. In 2021, the agency commissioned the establishment of the 'Client Forum', a network organisation of six separate organisations that advocates for the interests of children, young people and parents from an independent position and that aims to strengthen their voice at all levels.

Challenges in Flanders, Belgium

The child welfare sector faces challenges such as complex procedures, compartmentalisation, high thresholds and long waiting lists. In 2021, the government launched the aspirational initiative 'Early and near', aimed at creating an integrated family and child welfare policy. This aims to address eight challenges, which include the following. First, it is noted that the first 1,000 days of a child's life provide a unique opportunity for effective preventive family support. Second, it is noted that strengthening basic services such as daycare and schools, with prevention, early detection, early intervention, relapse prevention, and primary care support is crucial. Related to this, the third, fourth and fifth challenges are to ensure that services are local, that families have power and influence over the shape, focus, nature and delivery of those services, and that services are available for as long as necessary. The sixth challenge is to break the social taboo around child welfare and the seventh is to allocate scarce resources efficiently. Lastly, the eighth challenge is to design, deliver and evaluate services through innovative collaboration models and interorganisational collaboration. After a pilot phase in six regions, the rollout is planned from 2027.

Introduction to the country context: Northern Ireland

The partition of the island of Ireland in 1921, following the implementation of the Government of Ireland Act in 1920, gave rise to the area known as Northern Ireland. It is located in the northeast of Ireland. Its official languages are Irish and English, and it has an estimated population of 1,910,543. The partition of Ireland in 1921 reflects a long history of British colonialism, periods of conflict and the localised geographical segregation of communities, schools and other local community services. The creation of the partition caused further conflict. This culminated in a period known as 'The Troubles', which occurred from the late 1960s through to the signing of the Peace Agreement in 1998 and was marked by significant violence. Those directly involved in the conflict were Republican and Loyalist paramilitaries, and state forces. At least 50,000 people were killed or injured. The legacy of the Troubles continues today with periods of localised, intermittent violence, evidence of the ongoing segregation of some geographical areas and their services, and the ongoing influence in some localities of paramilitary groups. Child welfare professionals work in this challenging context to deliver child welfare services (Duffy et al, 2019; Campbell et al, 2021).

Positioning of child welfare services within the Northern Ireland policy structure

The Northern Ireland Executive, through the Department of Health, has overall responsibility for child welfare and other social care services (such as disability and mental health) which are all delivered at a local level through five integrated Health and Social Care Trusts, which have been in existence since 1973. Each Trust covers a different geographical area.

Currently the Children Order (Northern Ireland) 1995 provides the legislative framework that governs the response to and services provided for children and their families in need of support, and children at risk of harm and/or children who have suffered abuse and harm. New legislation, the Adoption and Children Act (Northern Ireland) 2022, is being implemented.

Statutory regulations which define and provide detailed guidance on the implementation of childcare law and the response of Health and Social Care Trusts to children and their families are premised on the following principles (Department of Health, 2017, para 1.5, p 10). First, the 'welfare of the child is paramount'. Reflecting the articles of the UNCRC, this means that an appropriate balance should be struck between the child's rights and parents' rights. All efforts should be made to work cooperatively with parents, unless doing so would be inconsistent with ensuring the child's safety.

Second, 'parents are supported to exercise parental responsibility and families helped to stay together'. Again, reflecting the principles of the UNCRC, this recognises that parents have responsibility for their children rather than rights over them. In some circumstances, parents will share parental responsibility with others, such as other carers or the statutory authorities. Actions taken by organisations should, where it is in the best interests of the child, provide appropriate support to help families stay together, as this is often the best way to improve the life chances of children and young people and to provide them with the best outcomes for their future. Third, there is the principle of 'partnership'. This recognises that safeguarding is a shared responsibility and the most effective way of ensuring that a child's needs are met is through working in partnership. Sound decision making depends on the fullest possible understanding of the child or young person's circumstances and their needs. This involves effective information sharing, strong organisational governance and leadership, collaboration and understanding between families, agencies, individuals and professionals.

In relation to making decisions, the fourth, fifth, sixth and seventh principles of 'prevention', 'proportionate responses', 'protection rights' and 'evidence-based decision making' are crucial. The principle of prevention recognises the importance of preventing problems occurring or worsening through the introduction of timely supportive measures. The principle of proportionality recognises that where a child's needs can be met through the provision of support services, these should be provided. Both organisations and individual practitioners must respond proportionately to the needs of a child in accordance with their duties and the powers available to them. This must be balanced against the protection of the child and in which decisions made are well informed and based on outcomes that are sensitive to, and take account of, the child or young person's specific circumstances, the risks to which they are exposed, and their assessed needs.

Lastly, underpinning and informing of all the principles outlined previously is that the 'voice of the child or young person should be heard'. This means that children and young people have a right to be heard, to be listened to and to be taken seriously, taking account of their age and understanding, and accommodating all the various ways in which children choose to express their views. Children should be consulted and involved in all matters and decisions which may affect their lives, and should be provided with appropriate, accessible information (in media of their choice) regarding the decisions being made. They must also be provided with support to do so where that is required. Where feasible and appropriate, activity should be undertaken with the consent of the child. Children must be informed about how and in what ways their own views have been considered and had influence. They must also be clear about their rights to representation and complaint.

Children's participation as a policy directive

In policy and practice, the legal obligations associated with the UNCRC are noted and underpin policy and practice principles. In the overarching statutory regulations, it is noted that all children, in line with their age and abilities, should be supported to understand the extent and nature of their involvement in plans and decisions that affect them (Department of Health, 2017, 2022). An outline of the various policies and practices can be found in a report by the Northern Ireland Commissioner for Children and Young People (NICCY, 2022).

Young children's participation in practice

All professionals are tasked with responsibility to promote, safeguard and protect the participation rights of children and to 'meaningfully engage them in decisions which contribute to meeting their needs, including their safeguarding needs' (Department of Health, 2017, para 5.1, p 37). This same section outlines that children should be supported to understand what services are available and why they are being provided; how they can be involved and how they can be helped to articulate their views, wishes, feelings and their own sense of the risks to which they are exposed and what they feel can done to keep them safe; how their views will be considered when decisions about services to be provided and their future are being made; what concerns professionals have about them; how safeguarding and child protection processes work; and why and how decisions which run contrary to their views have been made.

The section also says that:

> Children who lack capacity to express their views on a particular matter require more specific or personalised support, for example, advocacy and representation or communication support or the provision of interpreters for sign or other languages. This should be provided

based on the specific needs of the child or young person and consideration should be given to whether additional professional support should also be sought to assist other members of the family to express their views. (Department of Health, 2017, para 5.1, p 37)

Other relevant organisations that work with children involved in child welfare services, such as Voice for Young People in Care (VOYPIC) (a voluntary organisation advocating with and on behalf of children in care), the Northern Ireland Commissioner for Children and Young People (NICCY) (a publicly funded organisation which has the responsibility for protecting children's rights as defined in the UNCRC) and other advocacy and support services, all align with the UNCRC principles.

Challenges in Northern Ireland

In Northern Ireland child welfare services are experiencing multiple challenges, including increased demand (especially due to the cost of living crisis, the enduring impact of the COVID-19 pandemic and the legacy of the Troubles in Northern Ireland), a small workforce relative to demand, instability within the workforce, inadequate/patchy service provision, long waiting lists and poor interagency communication. All this has an impact on professionals being able to implement the participation rights of young children.

In response to the crisis, the Northern Ireland Executive, through the Department of Health, commissioned a review of children's social services (Department of Health, 2023). The review made several recommendations that are being considered and taken forward by various government departments. Specifically in relation to children's participation rights, the importance of children's participation rights was emphasised by the children who were consulted. They outlined some of the negative consequences of their participation rights not being respected, including fear, anxiety, trauma, loss of control, lack of continuity, and shock.

While the review itself did not explore very young children's participation rights specifically, the feelings identified by the children who were consulted are just as likely to be experienced by very young (including preverbal) children. The children consulted with offered ideas and approaches about how, when, in what ways and with what hoped-for outcomes they should be more centrally involved. It remains to be seen whether the outworkings of the review lead to fundamental and lasting changes in terms of the ways in which all children's participation rights – their expertise, experiences and views – are promoted, protected and safeguarded.

However, it remains the case that the participation rights of very young children remain an area that has not received specific attention, despite the deaths of very young children who were known to social services and other professionals. This requires urgent attention.

Introduction to the country context: Spain

Spain is a country whose territory is located mainly in the extreme southwest of Europe and the Canary Islands off the northwestern coast of Africa. It has an area of 505,370 km². According to the 2024 census, the Spanish population is 48,797875 inhabitants, with the Roma population being the most important ethnic minority, having been present in the territory since the 15th century.

Spain's form of government has been a parliamentary monarchy since 1978. Administratively it is divided into 17 Autonomous Communities (regions) and two Autonomous Cities, generating three levels of state organisation: local, autonomic and central (or state). The state is managed through exclusive, shared and delegated competences between the different levels. This means that the Autonomous Communities have full authority over certain areas of public life such as education, health and social services. However, the rights that are to be guaranteed in these areas are the same for all citizens.

The 20th century in Spain was marked by a civil war, 40 years of dictatorship and a period of transition to a democratic state. After the death of the dictator Franco in 1975, the country underwent significant changes. The 1978 Constitution guaranteed the equality of all citizens before the law, without distinction of ethnic origin. This is the basis for the protection of the rights of the Roma population in Spain and their gradual inclusion as full citizens.

The Roma population

The origin of the marginalisation of the Roma people in Spain goes back many centuries, with episodes of persecution and attempts at extermination. During the dictatorship, discriminatory practices based on stereotypes continued, keeping these people on the margins of society and limiting their opportunities for development. In this light of these exclusionary practices, Roma children have been deprived of basic rights such as education, health and housing.

The first years of democracy saw the inauguration of a social protection system that took the form of social services. One of the challenges of this new system has been the inclusion of the most vulnerable people, such as Roma, developing inclusive support policies to improve their living conditions and promote their full citizenship, guaranteeing their participation in society.

The participation of Roma children as a strategy for social inclusion in the social protection system in Spain

In this context, the concept of citizenship becomes important, especially that of active citizenship and, linked to this, of social participation. The latter refers to any action that citizens actively take in society – for example, participating in decision making in civic life (Council of Europe, 2023). Active citizenship refers to the ability to exercise rights and obligations, and to act in the social and political life of one's community. It implies real, reflexive, critical, dialogical and genuine involvement in social and political issues that concern citizens (Guichot, 2013; Save the Children, 2003). Social participation focuses on intervention in concrete issues, while active citizenship focuses on the individual's general engagement with the community.

The social participation of Roma children makes sense in itself as a right established in the UNCRC (1989). All children, including Roma children, have the right to take part in decisions that affect them, which requires access to decision-making spaces. Furthermore, the exercise of this right requires a certain amount of autonomy and information (Bolívar, 2016), which is acquired through civic pedagogy and consolidated through participation in civic life. To this end, participatory opportunities must be created from childhood, especially in 'any system that aspires to be democratic and particularly in those nations that already believe they are democratic' (Hart, 1993) because 'participation is one of those virtues essential for coexistence and good practice in multicultural and pluralistic societies such as today's' (Guichot, 2013, p 25). Participation is built and consolidated through being exercised by citizens. Without this, individuals are likely to feel increasingly excluded.

Child participation is a key to social change, especially in contexts of poverty and social exclusion. It is necessary to promote spaces for child participation that allow their needs, proposals and interests to be known and considered, and to transform them into actions.

Children's participation in practice

Social organisations such as Fundación Secretariado Gitano are committed to the social participation of Roma children in order to make their voices heard in those citizen spaces where they have traditionally had little representation. Participation is encouraged in socio-educational activities, where the children themselves make decisions about the rules and some of the content of the activity. There are also examples of collaboration with institutions such as the Madrid City Council that have created spaces for child participation such as the Councils for Child and Adolescent Participation, where children put forward proposals for the improvement of their communities that they have previously drawn up with their peers.

Key messages and a challenge in Spain

In conclusion, three key concepts and one warning are highlighted. The three concepts are that: first, social participation and active citizenship are elements of social inclusion; secondly, social participation requires learning and consolidation through practice from childhood onwards; and, third, the participation of Roma children requires spaces for participation where their voices are heard. Our warning is that there is a risk that child participation may be merely symbolic or tokenistic participation, with little or no impact, and that these processes are used as an institutional or political cover (Hart, 1993).

Introduction to the country context: Norway

Norway is an elongated country with approximately 5.5 million inhabitants, of which approximately 1.1 million are children under the age of 18. Of these, 47,000 children received help from Child Welfare Services in 2022 (Barnevern, 2022). The Indigenous population group, the Sami, make up a smaller percentage of the population. About 5–6 per cent of the population are immigrants or refugees from various other countries in the world. At the time of writing, Norway is divided into 15 counties and 357 municipalities. The long coastline of over 100,000 km ('Norges kyst og havområder', 2021) means that many children and families grow up with boats, fishing and activities related to coastal life. The capital city, Oslo, has 700,000 inhabitants.

The Norwegian political system is a representative democracy in which people vote directly in elections, and the representatives who are elected to the Storting, county councils and municipal councils govern on behalf of the people (Stortinget, nd). In the years after the Second World War, social democratic policy has prevailed. Publicly funded welfare schemes, political freedom and human rights are emphasised (Lange, nd). These schemes, together with tax income from wage earners, constitute a safety net for the many welfare schemes that exist, including public health and school systems, social security and pension schemes, child benefit for families with children, subsidised culture and leisure facilities for children, and full kindergarten coverage for all children from the age of one.

Positioning of child welfare services within the Norwegian policy structure

Responsibilities within the Norwegian child welfare system are split, with certain functions assigned to municipalities and others to the state. The municipal child welfare services proactively prevent, identify and address child neglect and abuse. They also initiate interventions to enhance the wellbeing of children and their families. The state agency, known as the Child, Youth and Family Directorate, has a special responsibility for managing childcare residential institutions and recruiting foster homes. In-home support, provided while the child lives with the parents, is most widespread. In 2022, this applied to 38,000 children, while only 8,000 were placed in alternative care settings (foster homes or institutions) (Barnevern, 2022). Children with immigrant backgrounds receive assistance more frequently than other children (Bufdir Barnevernstatistikk, 2022).

The child welfare services collaborate with other services (kindergartens, schools and health services) to improve each child's situation, and they work directly with children themselves and with parents as far as possible. In their work, child protection services must also consider the child's ethnic, cultural, linguistic and religious background, and the special rights of Sami children must be safeguarded.

Children's participation as a policy directive

When it comes to children's participation in child protection and child welfare practices, Norway has a clear policy that children should have a voice in decisions and actions that affect them and have their views taken into consideration. This approach to children as rights holders and respected human beings is reflected in the fact that Norway was the first country in Europe to have its own Child Welfare Act (in 1898) which has subsequently been revised several times, the last time being in 2021.

In 2003, the UNCRC (UN, 1989) was also incorporated into Norwegian law, and in 2014, children's rights were included in the Norwegian Constitution. It says: 'Children have a right to respect for their human dignity. They have the right to be heard in matters concerning themselves, and their opinion shall be given weight in accordance with their age and development' (Grunnlova, 1814, § 104). Similar wording can be found in the Norwegian Child Protection Act:

> A child who is able to form his own opinions has the right to participate in all matters concerning the child according to this Act. Children have the right to speak to child protection services regardless of their parents' consent, and without the parents being informed about the conversation in advance. The child must receive adequate and adapted information and has the right to express his opinions freely. The child must be listened to, and the child's opinions must be given

weight in accordance with the child's age and maturity. (Barnevernloven, 2021, § 1–4: 1.ledd)

The legislative framework highlights that children possess the capability to express their thoughts and emotions via verbal and nonverbal communication. It further clarifies that although children's participation is fostered, it should not be understood as providing them with the authority to make decisions on their own. Additionally, they are not obligated to partake in the participation process. The authorities highlight that there is a significant link between the consideration of what is in the best interests of the child – guided by the UNCRC, the Norwegian Constitution and the Child Welfare Act – and the child's right to have a say in matters affecting them (Prop.133 L, 2020–2021, pp 87 and 88). Decisions to move a child must be decided by a separate child protection and health board, and children have the right to visit their parents and others with whom they are connected after they have moved.

One notable difference in Norway is that the word 'love' has been incorporated into its legislation. The clause expresses that the needs of children and young people should be met with security, love and understanding (Barnevernloven, 2021 § 1–1: 1.ledd). The word 'love' in this context continues to be debated among professionals in child protection. Many argue that the term 'care' is more appropriate, but since the word 'love' is in place as a fundamental provision, the challenge goes to professionals to engage with vulnerable children in welfare settings in a way that expresses love for each individual child.

Another notable aspect of Norwegian children's policies is that they focus on obligations to take care of all children rather than just those who are vulnerable. In 1981, Norway became the first country in the world to enact the Children's Ombudsman Act. The law establishes that its primary task is to advocate for children's interests within society (Barneombudsloven, 1981) and to ensure that Norway upholds its commitments as per the

UNCRC (Barneombudet, nd). The Ombudsman has, among other things, advocated for the strengthening of children's right to participate in child welfare services, asserting that this right is violated far too often (Barneombudet, 2018). These regulations firmly establish the perception of children not only as significant individuals with inherent rights in the present but also as the pillars of our future democracy, entrusted with the responsibility of ushering in new eras for generations to come. Despite Norway's strong emphasis on welfare, political freedom and human rights, the country faces ongoing challenges regarding child welfare participation practices.

Young children's participation in practice and challenges in Norway

Even though Norway is recognised as a leading country when it comes to children's rights, care and upbringing, their right to participation in child protection and child welfare services is not always fulfilled in practice. The main challenges relate to the following. First, there is a 'lack of tailored communication' between children/youth and their contact person in child welfare. Second, there is a 'tendency towards formal rather than genuine participation'. Third, there is a 'lack of appropriate documentation practices'. Fourth, there are 'organisational barriers' to participation. Fifth, 'adult attitudes/lack of knowledge about different minorities' leads to misunderstandings and mistrust. Sixth, it is the case that 'very young children rarely get to participate' and, lastly, it is also the case that 'many children are unaware that they can have a trusted person with them in meetings with child welfare' (Nøkleby et al, 2024, p 5).

Conclusion

This chapter has briefly outlined the legal frameworks pertaining to child welfare and child protection in the countries involved in the PANDA project. While all countries are state signatories to the UNCRC (UN, 1989), there are differences in emphasis in terms of country-specific legal frameworks, reflecting contextual factors. These differences can also be seen in practice and the various approaches, methods and emphasis given to the participation rights of very young children. The next chapter focuses on the theoretical ideas and values informing the different approaches that seek to engage infants and young children in their fundamental right to express their views (verbally or non-verbally through gestures, movements and/or in any other way of the child's choice, preference and/or capacity) and to have their views considered.

References

Barneombudet (2018) 'Notat om høring om forslag til endringer i barnevernloven (bedre rettssikkerhet)'. Available at: https://www.barneombudet.no/vart-arbeid/brev-og-innspill/notat-om-horing-om-forslag-til-endringer-i-barnevernloven-bedre-rettssikkerhet (accessed 19 May 2025).

Barneombudet (nd) 'Barneombudets historie'. Available at: https://www.barneombudet.no/om-barneombudet/var-historie (accessed 19 May 2025).

Barneombudslove (1981) Lov av 6. mars 1981 Lov om Barneombud. Available at: https://lovdata.no/dokument/NL/lov/1981-03-06-5/%C2%A74#%C2%A74 (accessed 19 May 2025).

Barnevern (2022) 'Barn og unge med barnevernstiltak'. Available at: https://www.ssb.no/sosiale-forhold-og-kriminalitet/barne-og-familievern/statistikk/barnevern (accessed 19 May 2025).

Barnevernloven (2021) Lov av 18. juni 2021Lov om barnevern. Available at: https://lovdata.no/dokument/LTI/lov/2021-06-18-97 (accessed 19 May 2025).

Bolívar, A. (2016) 'Educar Democráticamente para una Ciudadanía Activa', *Revista Internacional de Educación para la Justicia Social*, 5(1): 69–87. https://doi.org/10.15366/riejs2016.5.1

Bufdir Barnevernstatistikk (2022) 'Barnevernstiltak til barn med innvandrerbakgrunn'. Available at: https://www.bufdir.no/statistikk-og-analyse/barnevern/barnevernstiltak-til-barn-med-innvandrerbakgrunn (accessed 19 May 2025).

Campbell, J., Duffy, J., Tosone, C. and Falls, D. (2021) '"Just get on with it": a qualitative of study of social workers' experiences during the political conflict in Northern Ireland', *The British Journal of Social Work*, 51(4): 1314–1331.

Council of Europe (2023, 28 September) 'Ciudadanía y participación'. Available at: https://www.coe.int/es/web/comp ass/citizenship-and-participation (accessed 19 May 2025).

Decreet betreffende de rechtspositie van de minderjarige in de integrale jeugdhulp (2019, 1 September). Available at: https://codex.vlaanderen.be/Portals/Codex/documenten/1013455.html (accessed 19 May 2025).

Department of Health (2017) *Co-operating to Safeguard Children and Young People in Northern Ireland*, Belfast: Department of Health.

Department of Health (2022) *A Life Deserved: Caring for Children and Young People in Northern Ireland*, Belfast: Department of Health.

Department of Health (2023) *The Northern Ireland Review of Children's Social Care Services. Children's Social Care Services Northern Ireland. An Independent Review*, Belfast: Department of Health.

Duffy, J., Campbell, J. and Tosone, C. (2019) *Voices of Social Work Through The Troubles*, Belfast: British Association of Social Workers Northern Ireland (BASW NI), Northern Ireland Social Care Council (NISCC).

Eerdekens, W., Aerts, L., Haedens, N., Heirbaut, E., Lowagie L. and Saenen, V. (2022) *Belgian Legal Framework and Policies on Child Welfare and Protection. Regulations and Practices. Brief for Practitioners.* Available at: https://reacch.eu/wp-content/uploads/2022/12/Belgian-legislations-on-child-welfare-and-child-protection_En-1.pdf (accessed 19 May 2025).

Grunnlova (1814) Lov av 17. mai 1814 Kongeriket Norges grunnlov. Available at: https://lovdata.no/dokument/NL/lov/1814-05-17-nn (accessed 19 May 2025).

Guichot, V. (2013) 'Participación, ciudadanía activa y educación', *Teoría de la educación*, 25(2): 25–47.

Hart, R. (1993) *La participación de los niños: de la participación simbólica a la participación auténtica*, Bogotá: Editorial Nueva Gente.

NICCY (Northern Ireland Commissioner for Children and Young People) (2022) *Statement on Children's Rights in Northern Ireland 3*, Belfast: NICCY.

'Norges kyst og havområder' (2021) Available at: https://www.regjeringen.no/no/tema/klima-og-miljo/naturmangfold/innsiktsartikler-naturmangfold/hag-og-kyst---behov-for-a-sikre-artsmangfold/id2076396/#:~:text=Norge%20har%20verdens%20nest%20lengste,med%20grunnere%20omr%C3%A5der%20n%C3%A6r%20fastlandet (accessed 19 May 2025).

Nøkleby H.L.L., Bergsund, H.B. and Johansen T.B. (2024) *Utfordringer for barn og unges medvirkning i barnevernet. En studie av forskningslitteratur og sentrale aktørers erfaringer*. Oslo: Folkehelseinstituttet.

Prop.133 L (2020–2021) *Lov barnevern (barnevernsloven) og lov om endringer i barnevernsloven*, Oslo: Barne- og familiedepartementet (Regjeringen Solberg).

Save the Children (2003) *Participar también es cosa de niños. Guía didáctica para el profesorado*. Valencia: Generalitat Valenciana. Available at: https://www.savethechildren.es/sites/default/files/imce/docs/guiaparticipacionvalencia.pdf (accessed 19 May 2025).

Stortinget (nd) 'Om Stortinget Folkestyre'. Available at: https://www.stortinget.no/no/Stortinget-og-demokratiet/Storting-og-regjering/Folkestyret/ (accessed 19 May 2025).

Turnell, A. and Edwards, S. (1997) 'Aspiring to partnership. the signs of safety approach to child protection', *Child Abuse Review: Journal of the British Association for the Study and Prevention of Child Abuse and Neglect*, 6(3): 179–190.

UNCRC (1989) *The United Nations Convention on the Rights of the Child*, Geneva: United Nations.

Vlaanderen (2024) 'Bekwaambeid'. Available at: https://www.rechtspositie.be/themas/bekwaamheid (accessed 19 May 2025).

FOUR

The participation rights of infants and babies

Wendy Eerdekens and Eva Heirbaut

Introduction

While we all have legal obligations to promote, protect and safeguard the participation rights of all children, regardless of their age, background and any other characteristics, we have found that the younger the child is, the less their participation rights are considered, and that this is especially the case regarding babies and infants aged 0–3 years. Despite the fact that young, preverbal children have often been excluded from participatory processes, there is growing evidence from a range of disciplines, including early childhood studies, education and infant mental health, that children can be included in participatory processes and practices (Lundy, 2019; Murray et al, 2019; Eerdekens et al, 2020–2023; Vliegen and Verhaest, 2021; Heirbaut and Eerdekens, 2022–2024; Singh, 2022).

The UNCRC (UN, 1989) does not set a minimum age for children's participation rights and within this framework (as noted in earlier chapters), all children, including infants and babies, have participation rights (Alderson et al, 2017; Alderson and Yoshida, 2019; Hultgren and Johansson, 2019; Lundy 2019). General Comments No. 7 and No. 9 provide a detailed analysis of the definition and implementation of these rights, highlighting the 'progressive exercise of rights', even for the very youngest children, which begins at birth (CRC, 2005). Some nations are further ahead than others in the implementation of the very youngest children's participation rights. In Scotland, for example, the UNCRC has been implemented into domestic law, and best practice guidelines called 'The voice of the infant' and an infant pledge have been published (Scottish Government, 2023). Other nations and their organisations have given this area less consideration. In this chapter, we attempt to answer the central question: how can we create an infant-friendly environment within child welfare that – if achieved – automatically promotes the participation rights of babies and infants? Our inspiration is drawn both from our involvement in the PANDA project and related research undertaken as part of an ongoing practice-oriented scientific project 'The Participation of Infants (0–3) in Child Welfare and Child Protection through Cross-sector Co-creation' (Heirbaut and Eerdekens, 2024).

How do we understand the terms 'infant' and 'babies'?

The term 'infant' is understood differently in different contexts. For example, professionals involved in child mental health in Flanders, Belgium, where we have undertaken some research in addition to the PANDA project, note that an infant can be understood as a child from conception to five years old. In the UK, before a baby is born, they are referred to as 'unborn child' or foetus and the term 'infant' means a child from birth to one years old, but can be extended to a child from birth to two years old. After two years old, a young child is referred to as a 'toddler', usually indicating that they are walking. In Norway, the term 'infant' means any child between birth and six months or two years old. In Spain, the term 'infant' refers to a child between birth and one year old. The term 'infant' becomes even more complicated because some jurisdictions have infant primary schools (for children aged between four and seven). The term 'baby' has a more commonly shared universal definition, meaning a very young child from birth to about 12–18 months old. The important point here is for all professionals to think about the meaning of the terms 'infant' and 'baby' in their own particular context because this has relevance when thinking of their participation rights. In this chapter on infants (aged from conception to three years old), we also focus on very young babies.

The relational and contextual elements of the participation rights of babies and infants

As noted in Chapter 2, the UNCRC and General Comments No. 7 and No. 9 remind us that babies and infants are social and emotional beings, and communicate through body language. Babies and infants are fascinating and are all unique. From their earliest encounters, they learn that they are part of a relational world. From the very beginning, parents and carers have the important task of learning to 'read' their baby's body language and to give words to what they see, as well as to the intentions they presume or the meanings they infer from the baby's signals (Vliegen and Verhaest, 2021). Babies and infants are also attuned and adjust their behaviour according to the signals from their parents and carers (such as their parent/carer being impatient and unreceptive or calm and receptive). This reciprocal and relational context between child and caregiver is highlighted by Winnicott (2004 [1952], quoted in Janson, 2018, para 3) who famously said: 'There is no such thing as a baby meaning, of course, that wherever one finds an infant one finds maternal care, and without maternal care there would be no infant.'

Winnicott (2004 [1952]) highlights that babies and infants are part of, relate to and participate in a social and relational reality. For example, in response to situations around them or their internal emotions, a baby or an infant expresses their needs and feelings in their own ways through facial expressions, body movements and vocalisations such as crying, gurgling, laughing, kicking their legs and waving their arms. We know too that some of these body movements also occur in the womb, including thumb sucking and reacting to their mother's voice. In this way, babies and infants (including prenatal babies in the womb during pregnancy) can be viewed as subjects.

Helpful conceptual frameworks

Relational autonomy

This perspective (Herring, 2014; McLaughlin, 2020; Riddell and Tisdall, 2021) centres on a social and relational, rather than an individualistic, view of humanity. Who the infant is, how much agency they have, how far they participate and in what ways and on what issues are determined by their relationships with their parents and caregivers. The concept enables an understanding of the intricacies of the participation of infants: the infant has agency over their own life, within the boundaries of their social, physical and mental state, and within their own social and relational context where they are dependent on their adult caregivers. For adults (professionals and parents) to respect and engage with the agentic capacity of babies and infants requires interaction and appropriate attunement (Metselaar and Smulders, 2017). Another helpful concept is 'mentalisation', which is identified as an essential skill to facilitate infant participation. This is explained further in the next section.

Mentalisation

Mentalisation means making sense of both one's own behaviour and the behaviour of others based on what we think their underlying feelings, thoughts, intentions and desires might be (Hutsebaut et al, 2021). Parental mentalisation refers to an interest in the inner world of the infant. It involves looking beyond the child's behaviour to understand what the behaviour communicates about their experiences, feelings and difficulties. Additionally, it requires the caregiver's emotional availability to help the child make sense of their own and others' behaviour, articulate feelings and tell stories about who they are. Parental mentalisation also involves staying in touch with one's own thoughts and feelings during interactions with the infant and recognising that these influence the child, and that one's own experiences may differ from those of the child. This is a significant task and a challenge for new parents. However, mentalisation is something caregivers do almost continuously. It is not a 'separate activity', but rather a continuous process running through their 'parental' actions (Vliegen and Verhaest, 2021).

Mentalisation facilitates the participation of infants because it provides a way to uncover the child's voice which is embedded in the relationship between the infant and caregiver, especially when the infant cannot yet express themselves verbally. It involves considering the meaning of the child's thoughts and feelings. However, this requires caution, as it is always just one interpretation. A person cannot verify through verbal dialogue with the infant whether the meaning attributed matches what they think and feel. It remains a hypothesis, an awareness of not knowing for sure.

Mentalisation is a unique and complex interplay between the caregiver and the infant. When this process does not go well, this may be due to one or more factors that influence each other: first, factors related to the parent (for example, postpartum depression and other mental health issues, substance misuse, unresolved trauma and prolonged relational problems); second, factors related to the child (such as cognitive disability, increased sensitivity, and issues with emotional and social regulation); and, third, factors embedded in the relationship (for example, insecure, ambivalent attachments or mismatch in the temperaments of a child and their carer, or a rather insecure, introverted parent combined with a very temperamental child).

What happens in the parent–child relationship (or at the dyad level) is, therefore, crucial. For a baby or an infant, too much stress and/or prolonged exposure to stress, especially from a young age, can negatively impact a baby's or infant's development in various domains, in both the short term and the long term. Stressful relationships can make a baby or infant vulnerable and support from social services might be necessary (Vliegen and Verhaest, 2021). Responses from professionals involved in the lives of the child require the same process of mentalisation as outlined earlier. The next section considers in further detail the opportunities and barriers for professionals in the processes and practices of mentalisation where the participation of babies and infants is necessary.

The context of child welfare and child protection

In the PANDA project, we noted that professionals have little time, space and support to engage in mentalisation. This was supported by our subsequent research, in which almost all interviewed social workers and policy officers indicated that they primarily encounter caregivers in very stressful circumstances, a situation that temporarily or permanently undermines or nearly eliminates their capacity for mentalisation (Heirbaut and Eerdekens, 2024). Stress and negative emotions affect the parent–child relationship, making it less natural for caregivers to be socially and emotionally available and to understand their child. This poses the risk of the baby's voice being overshadowed in the relationship.

Social workers have highlighted that heavy caseloads, and a lack of training and support, are barriers to being attuned to babies and infants, and that therefore these very youngest of children become 'invisible'. This view is supported in other nations. For example, in the UK, government reviews into the deaths of babies and infants at home who were known to social services have found that a number of different professional groups were at risk of overlooking the child as a subject in their own right and that the child was rendered invisible (Winter, 2011; Ferguson, 2017; Thomas and Winter, 2024). Social workers can address this in various ways in order to ensure that all babies and infants are seen, heard and considered: promoting awareness of the role of the supporting third party; sharing child care responsibilities (it takes a village to raise a child); developing observation skills; and practising child-centred assessment and child-centred interventions.

Awareness of the supporting third party

In the context of working with families where there are childcare concerns, the involvement of a social worker can be seen as a supporting third party. In this regard, rather than just observing the child–parent dyad, the social worker actively becomes involved in and supports the parental mentalisation processes, thereby improving alertness and sensitivity towards the baby or infant. In cases where parents/caregivers are so overwhelmed by their own emotions and concerns that they are (not yet) able to mentalise, the social worker serves as a role model for mentalisation through the process of modelling. For example, if a baby starts to cry, the social worker might pick the baby up, hold them in a way that the baby can see the social worker's face and speak with them: 'It's OK. Are you hungry? Let's see if it's some milk you want.' If this does not soothe the baby, the social worker might continue modelling by saying 'I see that you are not hungry. I wonder if you are too hot. Shall we take your jumper off? Let's see. What do you think about that? Does that help?' and so on. In so doing, the social worker both pays attention to how the baby or the infant is responding and helps the caregiver to focus on this as well, while also, through modelling, giving them ideas as to how they can mentalise.

Awareness of the multi-perspective: 'It takes a village to raise a child'

As illustrated earlier, parents/caregivers under stress often no longer have the mental space to be sensitive to their child's inner world and become isolated, having little or no available context. Beyond directly supporting parents to mentalise, the social worker can work with the parent to seek for alternatives in the context to highlight the baby's or infant's voice. We can never be completely certain about what goes on in the inner world of a child. Making this visible and actively expressing it through significant others such as someone from kindergarten, a family member, a neighbour or another child broadens and nuances the infant's voice. This can be done through recording encounters to capture an infant's voice and views.

Awareness of the importance of observing as a skill

Social workers also take on an observational role. The importance of observation, its role in professional practice, the awareness of bias in observation, and methods and techniques are explored by O'Loughlin and O'Loughlin (2014), and Fawcett and Watson (2016), for example. As Fawcett and Watson (2016) note, as our views of children and childhood have changed (see Chapter 2), so too has our emphasis on observation of babies, infants and their interactions with people and the worlds around them. At the heart of the social workers' approach in this area is the need to learn' to be' and 'not to do' (Fawcett and Watson, 2016, p 203). Social workers watch and listen to the signals the baby or infant gives during a conversation or interaction. In some organisations, social workers participate in daily activities such as bringing the child to daycare, feeding them or becoming involved in the sleep routines. In the following example, a detailed description of an observation is outlined. 'Sam' is a six-month-old baby with whom child welfare services are involved and where a foster care placement is being sourced.

Box 4.1: Social worker observing baby Sam (six months old) in a nursery setting

Following an order obtained by the court, the foster care service is tasked with finding a suitable foster family for Sam. The social worker is tasked with attending a nursery that Sam attends, so that he can get to know more about him. He intends to observe how he reacts to those around him and what his routine is. He is present for his feeding, cleaning and sleep routines. He observes how the keyworker connects *with* Sam, how he responds to her, what he likes, what he doesn't like. He notices that the keyworker is very careful with Sam, avoiding sudden movements and noises, which seem to make him anxious (noted by his body tensing up and little cries). The tone of the keyworker's voice is soft, she touches him, and she explains to him what she is doing, using words that she would use in everyday conversations. Sam is engaging through eye, body movements and soft noises. He seems content and relaxed.

Observing the intricacies of interactions and understanding the significance of responses (some of which can seem small and barely visible) is a skill required by all social workers. To assist in the development of this skill, some social work courses in the UK (Fawcett and Watson, 2016) include an observation placement in an early childhood setting and social workers use video recordings of parent–child interactions to review later with the caregivers. From a pedagogical perspective, these powerful methodologies, such as video-home training and video-interaction training (Eliëns, 2010; O'Loughlin and O'Loughlin, 2014; Fawcett and Watson, 2016), can be crucial in supporting the development of highly effective observations skills and in supporting the promotion of mentalisation.

Awareness of assessment as a child-centred process

In child welfare and child protection, ensuring the safety of the child is crucial, and assessment is the process by which decisions are made regarding safety and risk (Nembhard, 2019;

Dyke, 2023; Thomas and Winter, 2024). In the example given in Box 4.2, although Sam is a baby in a baby chair during the assessment process, the social worker physically positions him so that he is placed in the centre of the conversation and at the same eye level as the parents. On the basis of an assessment, decisions or recommendations need to be made – for instance, to the juvenile judge – regarding appropriate intervention, child placement, returning home or closing the case. Everyone's perspective is taken into consideration, but the child's best interests are paramount. Even with various perspectives considered, the infant themselves cannot verbally express what they want, what their behaviour signifies, and thus what is effectively in their best interests; it remains an interpretation by the social worker in which they balance up various options. Ultimately, a decision must be made based on nonverbal understanding of the baby or infant, which is in tension with the awareness that it is always a 'not-knowing'. The involvement of a supportive third party in the parent–child dyad can provide a stronger foundation for interpreting the baby or infant's voice and prioritising their best interests as much as possible.

Box 4.2: Social worker positioning baby Sam at the centre of a meeting involving parents

Sarah (a social worker) visits Sam's parents. They discuss parental concerns, including alcohol abuse, violence and debts they have. When arriving at the parents' house, the social worker notices that Sam is in his seat on the floor, and the parents are much higher up seated at a table together. Sam begins to cry. Sarah addresses the parents: 'Oh, Sam is sitting a bit low, isn't he?' To Sam, she says: 'Hey Sam, where are you? I can barely see you. Is it not good being so far from us? Shall I ask mummy and daddy if you can sit with us?' Sarah turns to the parents and looks at them kindly and questioningly. They say that they can't put Sam on a chair, that he's still too small. Sarah discusses with the parents how they can give Sam a more equal spot with them. They decide to put the baby seat on the table, meaning that Sam is at the same eye level as everyone else. Sam stops crying.

Risk, power and rights

In child welfare and child protection, concerns are usually multifaceted (Horwath and Platt, 2019). Often parents have their concerns, such as financial, housing and health issues, and relational problems. The safety of the child is paramount, but it is not always easy to work participatively with very young children living in stressful and unpredictable situations. A very young child might be distressed, unsettled, difficult to soothe, or very withdrawn, watchful and anxious. For the social worker, the challenge is: 'What do we do with this?' The UNCRC reminds us of the importance of parents and caregivers, and the dependence of the child on the parent/caregiver for their development. Thus, for social workers, it is crucial to remember that it is through the parent/caregiver that we come to know the child (Mainstone, 2014; Horwath and Platt, 2019). This power dynamic is important to be aware of and to negotiate in careful ways.

One way of doing so is by ensuring parental support. Articles 18 and 27 UNCRC remind us that caring for the parent/caregiver is caring for the child, and both articles outline our obligations to provide support services for parents to help them care for their children. However, there is a risk that the very young child becomes invisible and is 'out of sight' (Ferguson, 2017). For example, meetings might be held where the baby or infant is rarely present, and discussions might become dominated by parents/caregivers talking about their concerns. Another way is working in a child-centred way. This goes beyond merely applying certain methods from time to time; it involves a genuine belief in their competences and rights, and a continuous effort to give them control over their own lives, appropriate to their age and development.

Creating a baby/infant friendly organisational context: suggestions for the future

Micro-level: an individual mindset/attitude

As with participation in general, a participatory attitude is required. With babies and infants, this is characterised by a stance of not knowing, by probing, exercising caution and formulating different hypotheses. It requires social workers to have a strong reflective attitude, where asking questions takes precedence over making statements. Social workers should talk with babies and the infant, and provide information, even if the words are not understood by the child. This demonstrates an awareness and respect for the child as a full human being. This sets the tone and gives the child a meaningful position in the interaction (Vliegen and Verhaest, 2021). However, interaction is not only verbal. With babies and infants, social workers should pay attention to the analogue aspects of communication: the sensory experience, the acts of touching and being touched, the emotional content of interactions and body language (a happy face and good, direct eye contact, for example).

Social workers should establish and be respectful of the daily rhythms of babies and very young children – for example, what time are they fed, what time do they have their naps, what happens in their daily routine. By mentalising, social workers can become better attuned, co-regulate with the baby or infant, and support the parent and/or child in navigating their wider context (Reacch.eu, nd; Lowagie, 2023).

Meso-level: respect for the parent/caregiver–child dyad

Social workers should always remember that building a rapport and developing a relationship with a baby or infant always occurs through the parent/caregiver–child dyad. This means that the social worker approaches every baby or infant via the parent, and respect is needed here. This can be shown by the social worker asking for parental/caregiver permission to touch the child and/ or asking the parent/caregiver what they think their very young child is trying to convey though their gestures, noises and body language. In so doing, the social worker operates in and near the parent–child dyad and also strengthens this dyad by helping the parents/caregivers to mentalise. The UNCRC reiterates this approach, in that rights are contextual and contingent, relying on relationships with and through others (in particular parents) for their enactment and their effect.

Macro-level: infant-friendly organisations

There are some excellent examples of professionals respecting the participation rights of babies and infants. Often these good examples still depend too much on individual social workers and there is an overreliance on that one colleague known for their interest in working in participatory ways with babies and infants. To scale up these practices to an organisational level so that they become the 'norm' and embedded requires incorporating the baby/infant participation practice tips based on the principles and points outlined in Table 4.1.

Infant-focused policy

The implementation of regulations and policies will help in developing a baby/infant-friendly climate. While there is increasing policy attention on infants and babies, often the focus still seems to be on safety and risk. Sometimes, there is no mention of the participation rights of babies and infants. Protecting babies and infants relies on balancing children's protection, provision and participation rights. The approach is holistic and interrelated. One dimension does not exist in isolation from another. For social workers and organisations, it is crucial that their actions and the time devoted to babies and infants, along with being given time and tools, are facilitated and valued by policy.

Table 4.1: Practice tips for ensuring that the voices of babies and infants are heard and considered

Relationships	How are babies and infants supported? For example, is there continuity of care when the child is transported to appointments, to a new foster home, during contact arrangements?
Space	Is the space designed to be baby and infant-friendly? In social work offices, the environment is often set up with adults or older children in mind, sometimes overlooking the very youngest children. Spaces should be looked at through the eyes of a baby or infant: what does the baby or infant see when they enter the room from their own eye level; are there facilities and toys reflective of the preferences and needs of babies and infants, including the basics, such as a changing mat? (Vliegen and Verhaest, 2021)
Recording and documentation	How is the voice of the baby or infant recorded and documented – for example, does the baby or infant have their own file?
Representation	How is a baby/infant's voice included during meetings and discussions? Are there methods to support and ensure this (such as photographs, videos and a space for the child at the table, even if they are not physically present)? How is the baby/infant's voice incorporated into reporting?
Training and support	Are there opportunities for professionals to receive training and peer learning? Are there mechanisms for assessing the training and support needs of professionals?
Reflective spaces	Are there opportunities for professionals to reflect on the challenges and successes in honouring the participation rights of babies and infants?

Conclusion

The development of positive attitudes towards the capacities of babies and infants, the development of good methods, tools and practices, and the development of baby/infant-focused policy based on scientific insights will help ensure that the participation rights of our youngest children are honoured and respected. This, in turn, will contribute to the development of children who are self-assured and confident because they will have experienced that from the very beginning of their lives, their voice matters and they are a full member of a society. The next chapter outlines specific methods and tools that can help achieve these aspirations and promote the participation rights of our very youngest children.

References

Alderson, P. and Yoshida, T. (2019) 'Babies' rights, when human rights begin', in J. Murray, B. Swadener and K. Smith (eds) *The Routledge International Handbook of Young Children's Rights*, Abingdon: Routledge, pp 29–40.

Alderson, P., Hawthorne, J. and Killen, M (2017) 'The participation rights of premature babies', *International Journal of Children's Rights*, 13: 31–50.

Dyke, C. (2023) *Writing Analytical Assessments in Social Work*, Abingdon: Routledge.

Eerdekens, W., Heirbaut, E., Winter, K., Dahlø Husby, I., Juul, R., Mc Cafferty, P., Mercado García, E., Aerts, L., Haedens, N., Lowagie L., Saenen, V., Blanco Carrasco, M., Leyra Fatou, B., Corchado Castillo, A. and Dorado Barbe, A. (2020–2023) *Challenges and Possibilities Regarding Children's Participation. Brief for Social Workers*. Available at: https://reacch.eu/wp-content/uploads/2023/06/Challenges-and-possibilities.pdf (accessed 19 May 2025).

Eliëns, M. (2010) *Babies and Toddlers in the Picture: About Attuning, Interaction and Communication with Vulnerable Children*, Amsterdam: SWP.

Fawcett, M. and Watson, D. (2016) *Learning through Child Observation*, London: Jessica Kingsley.

Ferguson, H. (2017) 'How children become invisible in child protection work: Findings from research into day-to-day social work practice', *British Journal of Social Work*, 47(4): 1007–1023.

Heirbaut, E. and Eerdekens, W. (2024) *Participatie van Infants (0–3) in de Jeugdhulp via Sectoroverschrijdende Cocreatie*, Ghent: Artevelde University of Applied Sciences.

Herring, J. (2014) *Relational Autonomy and Family Law*, Dordrecht: Springer Science & Business Media.

Horwath, J. and Platt, D. (2019) *The Child's World: The Essential Guide to Assessing Vulnerable Children, Young People and Their Families*, 3rd edn, London: Jessica Kingsley.

Hultgren, F. and Johansson, B. (2019) 'Including babies and toddlers: A new model of participation', *Children's Geographies*, 17(4): 375–387.

Hutsebaut, J., Nijssens, L. and van Vessam, M. (2021) *De Kracht van Mentaliseren*, Amsterdam: Boom

Janson, S. (2018) 'Winnicott. Zijn leven. Zijn werk. Een Theorie?', *Tijdschrift voor psychoanalyse & haar toepassingen. Jaargang*, 24(1). Available at: https://www.tijdschriftvoorpsychoanalyse.nl/inhoud/tijdschrift_artikel/PA-24-1-2/Winnicott (accessed 19 May 2025).

Lowagie, L. (2023) 'Foster care' (podcast). Available at: https://reacch.eu/media-library/interviews/ (accessed 19 May 2025).

Lundy, L. (2019) 'Implementing the rights of young children', in J. Murray, B. Swadener and K. Smith (eds) *The Routledge International Handbook of Young Children's Rights*, Abingdon: Routledge, pp 14–28.

Mainstone, F. (2014) *Mastering Whole Family Assessment in Social Work*, London: Sage.

McLaughlin, J. (2020) 'Relational autonomy as a way to recognise and enhance children's capacity and agency to be participatory research actors', *Ethics and Social Welfare*, 14(2): 204–219.

Metselaar, S. and Smulders, Y. (2017) 'Ook de Autonome Mens is Niet Alleen'. https://www.trouw.nl/nieuws/ook-de-autonome-mens-is-niet-alleen~b0102cfb/?referrer=https://www.google.com/

Murray, J., Swadener, B.B. and Smith, K. (eds) (2019) *The Routledge International Handbook of Young Children's Rights*, Abingdon: Routledge.

Nembhard, E. (2019) *Child and Family Assessment: Assessment Notebook for Children Social Worker*s, Independent Publishing.

O'Loughlin, M. and O' Loughlin, S. (2014) *Effective Observation in Social Work Practice*, London: Sage.

Reacch.eu (nd) 'Toolkit for trainers. Part 2: Challenges and possibilities'. Available at: https://reacch.eu/training-and-resources/ (accessed 19 May 2025).

Riddell, S. and Tisdall, E.K.M. (2021) 'Transforming children's rights? Dilemmas, challenges and implementation', *Journal of Social Welfare and Family Law*, 43(1): 1–7.

Scottish Government. (2023, 22 March) 'Voice of the infant: Best practice guidelines and infant pledge'. Available at: https://www.gov.scot/publications/voice-infant-best-practice-guidelines-infant-pledge/ (accessed 10 October 2024).

Singh, B. (2022) *Van Hart tot Hart. Inspiratie Vanuit het Jonge Kind*, Kalmthout: Pelckmans

Thomas, N.P. and Winter, K. (2024) *Social Work with Young People in Care: Looking after Children in Theory and Practice*, Abingdon: Routledge.

UNCRC (United Nations Committee on the Rights of the Child) (1989) *The United Nations Convention on the Rights of the Child*, Geneva: United Nations.

UNCRC (2005) *General Comment No. 7 (2005): Implementing Child Rights in Early Childhood,* 20 September 2006, CRC/C/GC/7/Rev.1, Geneva: United Nations.

Vliegen, N. and Verhaest, Y. (2021) *Vroege Ontwikkeling alle Kansen Geven*, Kalmthout: Pelckmans.

Winnicott, D.W. (2004 [1952]) 'Anxiety associated with insecurity', in *Through Paediatrics to Psychoanalysis, Collected Papers*, London: Karnac Books, pp 97–100.

Winter, K. (2011) 'The UNCRC and social workers' relationships with young children', *Child Abuse Review*, 20(6): 395–406.

FIVE

Creative participatory approaches, methods and tools

Esther Mercado Garcia and Elin Hassel Iversen

Introduction

The United Nations Convention on the Rights of the Child (UNCRC) (UN, 1989) gives every child a right to participate and be heard. To be seen and heard is essential to all humans. To be given a voice can help the child to find his or her language for self-expression. Children in protective systems need trusting and lasting relationships with adults who care for them. Therefore, professionals must adapt their processes and language to the inner world of children so that their thoughts and feelings can be spontaneously expressed (Wieder, 2017). In this context, the success of our engagement with children depends, in part, on our understanding and appreciation of the unique skills, talents and capabilities of each child. They live in a world of tangible realities and often express their experiences through play (Landreth, 2012). Adults attempting to understand children's lives and experiences often encounter asymmetries not only relating to age but also to communicative abilities. To overcome these, increasingly innovative approaches have been adopted (Butschi and Hedderich, 2021) and in this chapter we introduce a number of activities that can be used with young children in child welfare and child protection contexts.

The joy of participatory practice

A positive and trusted environment is joyful. The desire to do something together or to be with a special person is conveyed through inviting body language, smiling and making space for the invited person. If the invitation is overlooked, it leads to disappointment, but if it is accepted, joy becomes a part of the subsequent interaction: 'Performing joy is an initiative to joint play and a discreet questioning "Are you with me?" mirroring the idea of joy as a practice in children's peer relations' (Karjalainen, 2020, p 1659). Closely aligned to experiences of joy in participatory practices with children are ones of playfulness. Playfulness is an attitude or way of being, as opposed to a structured form of play. As such, it can be expressed outside a specific play-based intervention and, we argue, it needs to be the mindset of all practitioners seeking to engage children in participatory ways. As such, playfulness is a foundational professional disposition in participatory spaces and overcomes concerns that professionals in such spaces need to have therapeutic trainings. This is not the case. What is needed is a playful approach to participation, as noted in the example of Andreas and a professional named Clara in Box 5.1.

Box 5.1: Professional playfulness with children

Andreas, two years old, and Clara, the professional working with him, are pushing toy cars on the floor, past each other and up and down a small hill they have made. Then they park the cars, backing them into place one by one. Clara finds a figure and puts it in the parking lot. While moving the figure she is saying: 'Coffee, coffee, come and buy coffee.' Andreas looks at the professional, picks a figure and comes to buy coffee. Then they drive the cars again and park. Spontaneously, Andreas takes another figure and says: 'Ice cream, ice cream, come and buy ice cream.' The two of them burst out laughing.

The play, in the example of Andreas and Clara, occurs within the context of the available toy cars and figures. The development of the play depends on joyful interaction between the pair, which is linked to their ability to create new situations and introduce new elements, while the ending remains open. The experience of interaction in play is equally shared by all involved. The power balance between Clara and Andreas is levelled out because both the child's and the adult's initiatives and participation must be positively accepted by their play partner to create the necessary intersubjective relationship (Husen, 2022). Through play, children learn to: respect themselves and that their feelings are acceptable; express their feelings responsibly and assume responsibility for themselves; be creative and resourceful in confronting problems; have self-control and self-direction; and make choices and be responsible for their choices (Landreth, 2012, pp 87–89).

Broad approaches to creative and participatory engagement

The use of creative approaches in social intervention practices has gained significant relevance not only in relation to their impact on children's emotional, cognitive and social growth but also as tools that enhance the effectiveness of professionals' communication. Through the application of various methods, children express their feelings and thoughts nonverbally, promoting their participation (Robinson, 2006; Smith and Pellegrini, 2013; Lillard et al, 2013; Goldberg, 2017). Creative methods are based on inventive and imaginative processes. They can serve as constructivist tools to help participants describe, analyse and make sense of their experiences (Veale, 2005). There are several creative approaches, which can be classified as follows.

Art-based creative approaches are often connected with art-based therapy, which utilises visual arts to help children express their emotions and enhance psychological wellbeing. Engagement in artistic activities fosters cognitive and motor skills, creativity and problem-solving abilities (Coholic, Eys and Lougheed, 2012). It provides a particularly beneficial outlet for children who struggle to verbalise their thoughts, feelings and complex emotions, facilitating emotional release and understanding (Malchiodi, 2013). Moreover, it is effective in helping children recover from trauma by providing a safe space to explore and process their experiences (Bosgraaf et al, 2020).

Play-based creative approaches are usually connected with play therapy, which uses play to help children communicate, express feelings and solve problems. The nondirective nature of play therapy fosters a strong therapeutic alliance between the child and the therapist (Landreth, 2012). It is a child-centred approach that uses toys, games and imaginative play. Play allows children to naturally and engagingly process emotions and experiences (Bratton et al, 2005). It has been effective in addressing behavioural issues by providing a safe space for children to express and resolve conflicts (Ray et al, 2005).

Storytelling and dramatisation-based creative approaches use role-playing, storytelling and theatrical techniques to help children explore their emotions, improve their social skills and boost their self-esteem. Theatre provides children with a dynamic way to express their inner thoughts and feelings, promoting greater self-awareness (Jones, 2007). Through role play, children learn empathy, perspective-taking and social problem-solving skills (Corbett et al, 2016), enhancing their confidence (Lee, 2015).

Similarly, storytelling involves using narrative techniques to help children make sense of their experiences, develop their reading and writing skills, and enhance their imagination. Storytelling enriches vocabulary and comprehension skills, promoting overall language development (Isbell et al, 2004). It stimulates imagination and creative thinking, encouraging children to explore different perspectives and ideas (Jones and Pimienta, 2020). Sharing stories from diverse cultures fosters cultural awareness and empathy (Collins and Cooper, 1997).

Music and movement-based creative approaches are often associated with music therapy. Music and the adapted use of musical elements for nonmusical purposes have a profound impact on social and emotional development, improving social skills (Williams, Dingle and Clift, 2018; Glew, Simonds and Williams, 2021), communication (Geretsegger et al, 2014) and regulation, helping children manage their emotions, reduce their anxiety and improve their mood (Bieleninik et al, 2017; Mayer-Benarous et al, 2021). Such activities include singing, dancing and playing instruments.

Currently, there is advocacy for integrated approaches or the combination of multiple creative methods to enhance effectiveness and address children's needs in a holistic manner (Malchiodi, 2008; Oaklander, 2006). In this chapter, we aim to answer the following questions: do creative methods make it possible to place children in active roles within the social intervention process? What are the implications of using creative methods in professional practice? Can creative methods reduce the complex relationship between questions of power, control, responsibility and social intervention? What follows is an outline of various methods and tools that can be used by professionals working with children, explaining some of the advantages of their use, illustrated by some examples to serve as a guide.

Tools and methods in detail

The relationship between a professional and a child relies on the ability to comprehend the child's communication and foster an environment that encourages free expression. Choosing tools that facilitate clear understanding for professionals and enable children to explore real-life themes and creative expression through play helps establish effective communication (Landreth, 2012).

Sandplay therapy (see Figure 5.1) is a specific form of play therapy (Russo, Verman and Wolbert, 2006). This technique has been extensively used in assessment and therapeutic work, allowing for the creation of three-dimensional scenes using a variety of figures (Dale and Wagner, 2003; Hong, 2010). Margaret Lowenfeld was the first person to develop the World Technique, often known as 'sandplay', in the late 1920s due to her frustration with the limitations of traditional talk therapy in the psychoanalytic tradition. She named it the World Technique because 'World' was the word a child had used to describe what they had created with the sand and toys.

Sandplay provides a space for children to express their thoughts, feelings and reflect upon them (Lowenfeld, 1979, 1991, 2004). However, Dora Kalff significantly expanded this approach, emphasing the importance of attending to client interests and collaborating to provide activities for emotional release and various forms of therapeutic artistic expression (such as painting and clay sculpting) as a supplement to sandtray work (Kalff, 2003; Pearson and Wilson, 2019). The technique requires a sandbox of about 500 square inches and a diverse assortment of figures and objects for play. These should include people, animals, vehicles, buildings and vegetation to create various scenarios and contexts, as well as magical items and characters (see Figure 5.1). Children are free to construct as they wish, to choose figures and to use them to let the figures engage in their own fantasy (Kalff, 2003; Russo et al, 2006; Roesler, 2019).

The process of engaging in sandplay is often accompanied by three stages, as described by Allan and Berry (1993, cited in Russo et al, 2006). These stages (chaos, struggle and resolution) unfold over multiple sandplay sessions. Chaos reflects emotional turmoil in the client's life and may be characterised by placing many objects in the tray without apparent structure. This stage may occur during the first sandplay session or continue over several sessions, depending on the intensity of distressing emotions present. In the struggle stage, battles initially occur without a winner, but may gradually organise until a hero emerges, symbolising the mastery of good over evil. Finally, in the resolution stage, life returns to normalcy with a balance among the figures or the placement of figures in their appropriate habitats. It is during this stage that the client may demonstrate a sense of wholeness, fulfilment or integration of previously chaotic emotions (cited in Russo et al, 2006, pp 230–231).[1]

Toys and materials for the playroom: Professor Garry Landreth is internationally recognised for his writings and work with children. He offers a range of games and materials that allow children to fully express and explore their personalities and inner emotional world.[2]

Puppets are useful pedagogical tools with a longstanding relationship in early childhood education, playing a cherished role in children's learning and development (Karaolis, 2023).

Figure 5.1: A home therapeutic sand tray for individual use over time

Source: Photo by Elin Hassel Iversen

A puppet is defined as a movable inanimate object or figure controlled by strings or rods, or by placing the hand inside its body (Ahlcrona, 2012; Belfiore, 2013). It is a mobile doll manipulated by the puppeteer. The body movements provide visual impressions; a puppet conveys emotions and thoughts through movements, such as its hands and head. A puppeteer can also give voice to the puppet. In the hands of a puppeteer, a puppet is an inanimate object that comes to life (Kröger and Nupponen, 2019). There are various types, from finger puppets to hand puppets, glove puppets, rod puppets and shadow puppets. The expressiveness and dramatisation of puppets have not only entertained people but have also been used for education, information (Belfiore, 2013) and working with children with disabilities (Syabila and Irvan, 2023).

The use of puppets has proliferated in educational contexts. The Union Internationale de la Marionnette (UNIMA) https://www.unima.org/en/ is the oldest international theatre organisation in the world and provides a platform to exchange and share between people who practise puppetry (amateur or professional), work on this art (researcher, historians.) and/or are passionate about this art. Kröger and Nupponen (2019) demonstrate that the benefits of puppets are linked to: (1) generating communication; (2) supporting a positive classroom climate; (3) enhancing creativity; (4) fostering cooperation and integration into a group; and (5) changing attitudes.

Råde (2021) provides a comprehensive literature review on puppets in therapeutic contexts. It indicates that the first documented use of puppets with children in a therapeutic context was in 1936, when puppet shows were used to address behavioural issues. Puppets have also been used in hospital settings to help children cope with illness, verbalise feelings and learn about diseases. Puppets have also been utilised in group and family therapy. This review also suggests, based on other studies, how to choose puppets. The child-centred approach of play therapy, which emphasises a nondirective, trustworthy, and close relationship with the child, shares similarities with the child's perspective in modern early childhood education and care pedagogy (Råde, 2021, p 25).

The puppet is an object that comes to life being led by the puppeteer. In the communication, the puppet becomes the common third (Husen, 2022) and the puppeteer makes an indirect conversation through the puppet which has a name, a personality, a voice, nonverbal language and feelings. The puppeteer is using a hand puppet and must keep his or her head's position the same as the puppet when playing to make the illusion of a living character. The puppet is positioned between the child and the puppeteer so that the puppeteer can focus on the puppets head positions when playing and see the child behind the puppet.

Box 5.2: Puppets in practice

The puppeteer lifts the puppet: his body language is shy. The puppet looks at the child through his fingers. When the child looks back, the puppet looks down. Then the puppet looks at the child again and says: 'Hi', looks down again, lifts his head and says 'I am Aron'. Then the puppet looks at the puppeteer and she says: 'I am Linda', and when the puppet looks back at the child again the child says: 'Harry, my name is Harry'.

Aron:	You go to school?
Harry:	Yes.
Aron:	Me too, I am five years old.
Harry:	I am five years old too.
Aron:	(Happy) We are the same. (Pause) Do you like school?
Harry:	Not so much …
Aron:	(Careful) Are there bullies in your school too?
Harry:	Yes.
Aron:	(Afraid) They try to scare us, what can we do?
Harry:	I have stopped going to school.
Aron:	(Desperate) Then they win. (Pause) (Unsure) Is that right, that they can decide if we go to school or not?
Harry:	No, but … (pause)
Aron:	One time, (lowers his voice, whispers) I peed in my pants because I was so afraid.
Harry:	Did you tell the teacher? (Conversation continues)

After the introduction and presentation, the puppeteer addresses the problem. Now it is two boys equally talking. Aron the puppet can shift his personal feelings all the time, and if he plays a personal low status (Johnstone, 1987), he might lead Harry to take a personal high status and thereby hand over the lead of problem solving to Harry. Aron can say something funny if he likes. He can be in need of comforting. He can ask questions, and he can comfort Harry. It is important that Harry feels comfortable in the situation and the puppeteer sums up afterwards what the next problem-solving step is.

In another example, a puppet show takes place in a shoebox to help children consider complicated themes (see Figures 5.2 and 5.3). The puppeteer performs a short show of 5–10 minutes in a shoebox using puppets made of paper which are glued to sticks. After the show, the puppeteer and the therapist have a conversation with the child about the characters' experiences in the play and how they managed to

Figure 5.2: Teater Fusentast: performing in a box

Source: Photo by Ole Tolstad

Figure 5.3: Teater Fusentast: inside the box

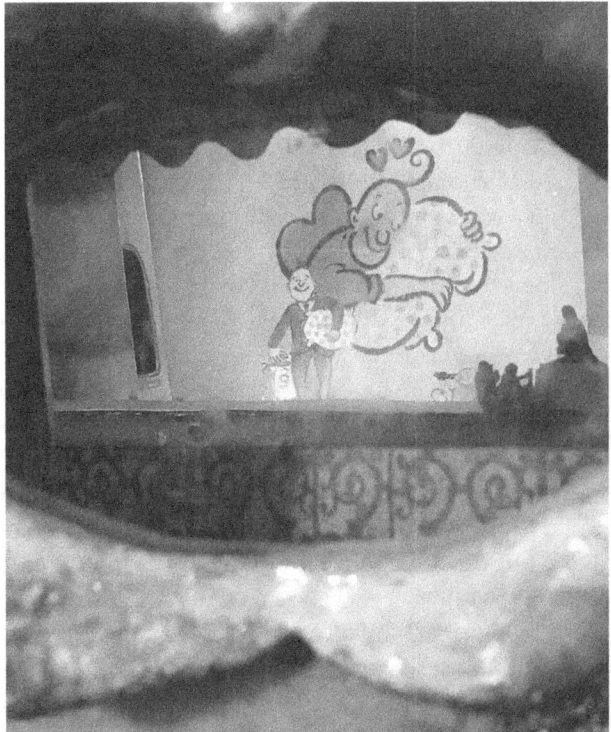

Source: Photo from Teater Fusentast

solve the problems that arose. This child-centred approach using basic materials (shoebox, paper and pencils) helps some children visualise and work on their own story together with the therapist. Transferring feelings to the paper puppets might give the space for mediation and reflection.

The Mosaic technique (using photo documentation and photovoice) was developed during a research study to include the 'voice of the child' in an evaluation of a multi-agency network of services for children and families, but subsequent discussions with practitioners through conferences and workshops have led to its use by early years practitioners (Clark, 2005). The idea behind the Mosaic approach is that professionals collect data through a wide range of means. These are what Clark and Moss consider 'individual tiles'. It is then the professionals' task to put these individual pieces together to form one big picture, just like many little tiles are formed into one big mosaic.

Clark and Moss's (2011) presentation of individual tiles in their book ranges from children's conferences and children's use of cameras, role plays, tours and mapping to conversations with relevant adults and caregivers. The individual tools or methods were chosen to enable young children to explore their experiences of being in an early childhood institution through talking, walking, making and reviewing. These forms of expression were chosen to be closely aligned with how young children might choose to communicate with friends and family (Clark and Moss, 2011). Clark (2005) refers to the methodological 'pieces' of the Mosaic approach (see Figure 5.4, adapted from Clark 2005, p 14). The development of the mosaic is based on three steps: stage 1 involves children and adults gathering documentation; stage 2 involves staff/adults and children piecing together information for dialogue, reflection and interpretation; and stage 3 involves deciding on continuity and change. Different methods are used, as illustrated in Figure 5.4.

These are the foundational tools; however, one is encouraged to explore other types of tools to complement each child's interests. It is important to note that applying a single method only gives the researcher one listening tool, so integrating methods from both stage 1 and stage 2 provides a complete 'pictured' documentation of the child's response and representation of his or her voice (Tan, 2019, p 69); stage 3 emphasises the applied nature of this approach to research with participants and is in keeping with adopting a participatory paradigm. Dialogue, reflection and interpretation have remained key features of working this way, but we have highlighted the relationship between listening and change.

Figure 5.4: Methodological 'pieces' of the Mosaic approach

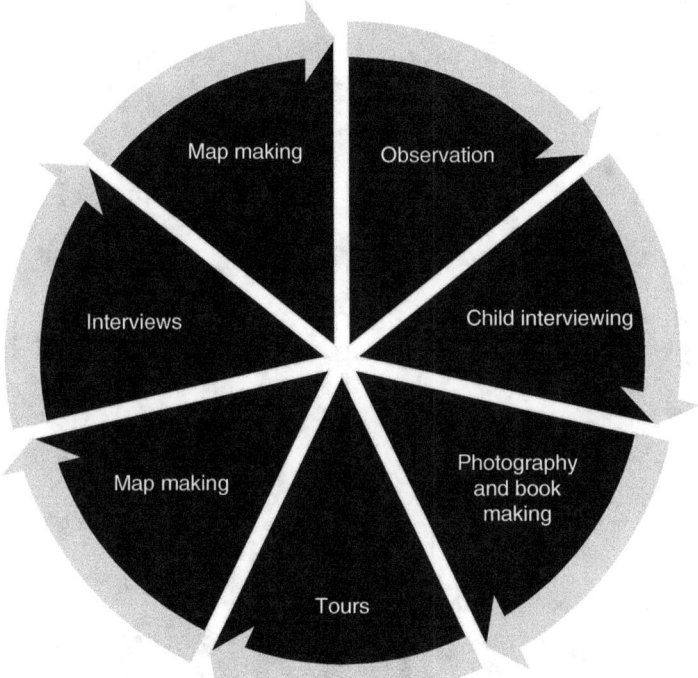

This acts as a reminder that listening is more than a tick-box activity to meet policy objectives (Clark and Moss, 2011).

Image theatre is a subset of forum theatre, a theatrical method developed by the Brazilian theatre artist, author and educator Augusto Boal, who saw theatre as a powerful tool for social change. In forum theatre performances, also called 'rehearsals for reality', various forms of oppression between people and society are highlighted, and the audience is always involved in creating the performances. Image theatre involves participants working together using their bodies to create still images or tableaux that depict feelings, situations and relationships (see Figures 5.5 and 5.6). These images

Figure 5.5: Image theatre work session at Ørland kulturskole, Norway

Source: Photo by Elin Hassel Iversen

Figure 5.6: Children in theatre

Source: Photo by Elin Hassel Iversen

can be processed in various ways. Interpersonal situations, such as violence, family life or friendship, are often well suited for this method.

There are several ways of working with image theatre. A facilitator, known as the 'joker', invites some of the participants to form a circle and from there each participant, without talking, steps into the centre and creates a sculpture that represents their impression of the theme that shall be worked on. When all participants have shown their still images one by one, the 'joker' asks the audience for alternative interpretations, and audience members step into the circle and show their impressions:

> As objects reflect the light that strikes them, so images in an organised ensemble reflect the emotions of the observer, her ideas, memories, imagination, desires ... The whole method of Theatre of the Oppressed ... is based on the multiple mirror of the gaze of others – a number of people looking at the same image, and offering their feelings, what is evoked for them, what their imaginations throw up around that image. This multiple reflection will reveal to the person who made the image its hidden aspects. (Boal, 2002, p 175)

In the first dynamisation, the 'joker' instructs everyone to come on stage and strike their poses simultaneously: 'As each participant connects with the image-making process, they are at-one-and-the-same-time agents and observers. By contributing to the image, they are simultaneously commenting on it' (Grant, 2017, p 192). From seeing all the subjective poses together, the image becomes objective, and what everybody is thinking is shown: 'The individual presentation of images gave us a "psychological" representation, now we are given a "social" vision; that is, we are shown how this particular theme influences or affects this particular community' (Boal, 2002, pp 177–178).

In the second dynamisation, the participants, at the 'joker's' signal, interact with each other's poses, creating a collective vision. In the third dynamisation, the 'joker' asks the participants to change their status from victim to oppressor (for example, from beggar to giver of alms). This stage allows participants to perform from their own subjective perspectives, portraying themselves and their perceived enemies.

The 'joker' asks a volunteer to illustrate the image made by the group by silently moving the bodies into other positions. When the image is finished, the 'joker' consults the group and the group collaborates to give information about changes to the 'joker', who moves the bodies into the places the group wants and then freezes the new image.

Drawing and painting: children's drawings are increasingly being used as a means of researching children's experiences because they give rise to possibilities for insight into children's individual experiences (Veale, 2005) and express emotions (Malchiodi, 2003; Stiles et al, 2010). The importance of using the artistic process in communication with children is fundamental in art therapy. The artistic process can provide another language, nonverbal or symbolic, through which they can unconsciously express feelings, desires, fears and core fantasies from their inner selves (Case and Dalley, 1990). It can be used as an emotion regulation technique (Brechet et al, 2020) and can be also used as an intentional teaching strategy to support children's development of executive function (EF) skills (Sonter and Jones, 2018). Case, Dalley and Reddick (2023) provide a wide array of techniques and theoretical perspectives on art therapy, with significant sections dedicated to using drawing in therapeutic settings with children (see Figures 5.7 and 5.8). The authors claim that the image is of great significance in the symbolic representation of inner experience – the emphasis on unconscious communication, the feelings, anxieties and concerns that surface through the artwork.

Moreover, Thrana et al (2023) explore how children's participation in a painting workshop can provide a space

Figure 5.7: Peacepainting

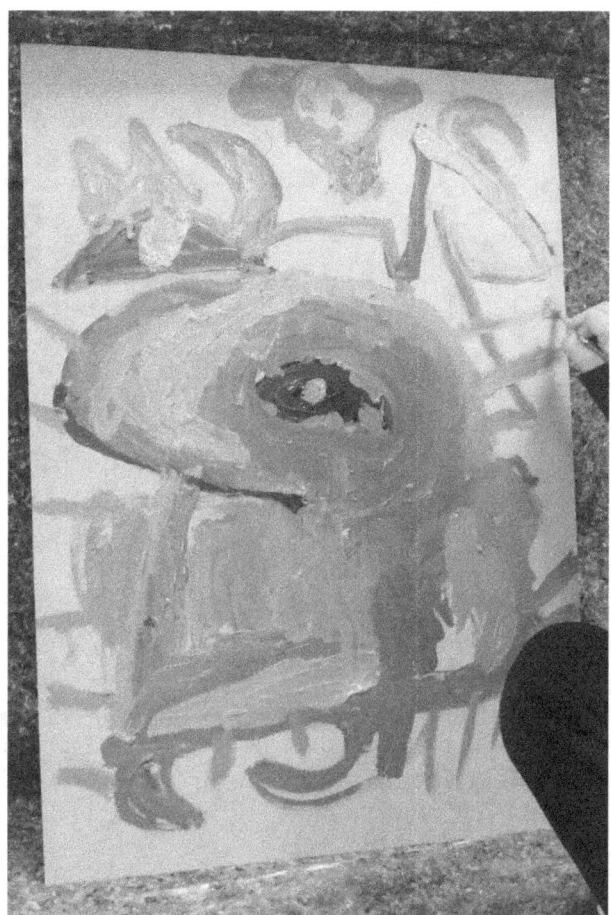

Source: Photo by Elin Hassel Iversen

for communication and social interaction in their home environment. The findings mainly show that the framework of the painting workshop, the peacepainting methodology and the social community among the participants enabled the children to engage in creative work and interaction.

Figure 5.8: Half water and half lava

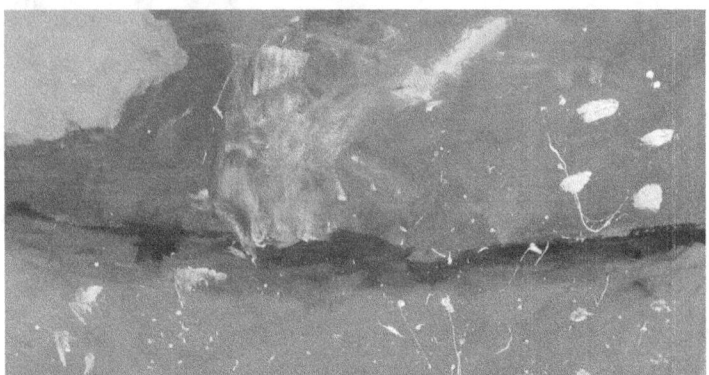

Source: Photo by Elin Hassel Iversen

To illustrate the impact of the painting workshop and the process for the children, Thrana et al (2023, p 323) have developed a model (see Figure 5.9) which highlights the change processes based on Wenger's three modes of belonging (alignment, imagination and mutual engagement). Practitioners might find this helpful in considering their own practice.

Recommendations for practice

Creative working methods can be implemented in the form of project work, where working with a theme aims to create an arena for exploration, curiosity and understanding. Children's interests and involvement must have a central place, and they should be able to influence pedagogical choices. Project work is a process-oriented activity that follows the dynamics that arise between the children and the theme or phenomenon on which they are focused. There is a close relationship between the actions and explorations of the adults and the children,

CREATIVE PARTICIPATORY APPROACHES, METHODS AND TOOLS

Figure 5.9: Change processes in painting workshops

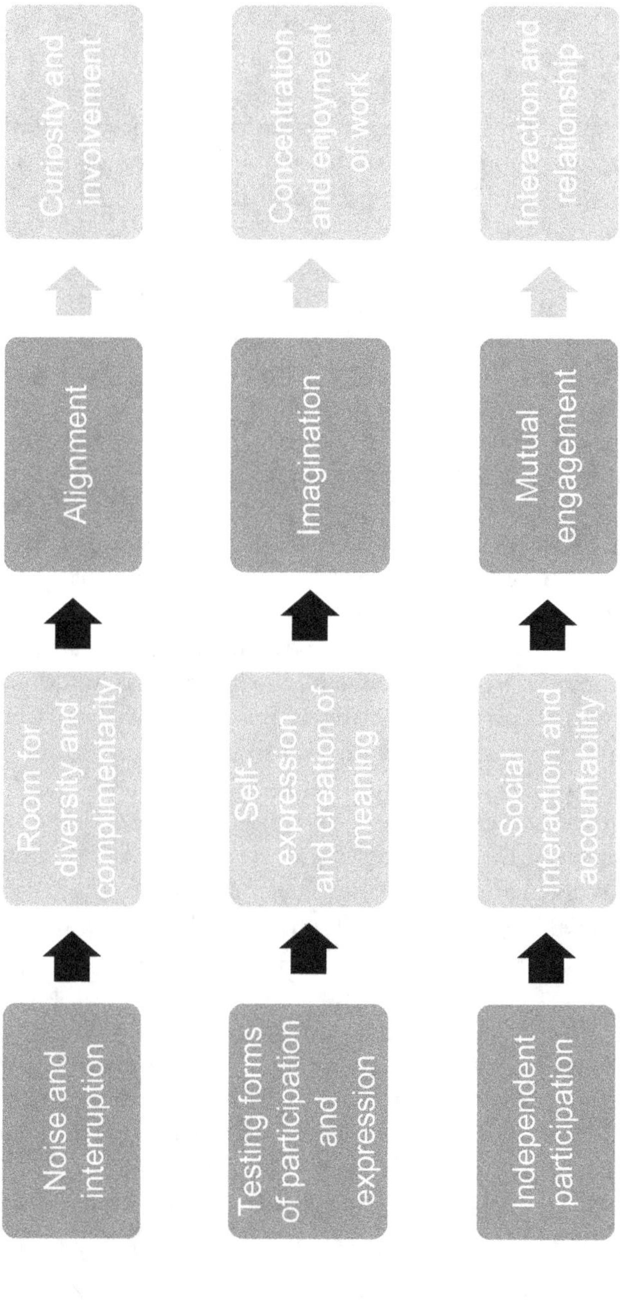

Noise and interruption	→	Room for diversity and complimentarity	→	Alignment	→	Curiosity and involvement
Testing forms of participation and expression	→	Self-expression and creation of meaning	→	Imagination	→	Concentration and enjoyment of work
Independent participation	→	Social interaction and accountability	→	Mutual engagement	→	Interaction and relationship

Source: Adapted from Thrana et al (2023)

which are mutually dependent on each other (Norwegian Directorate for Education and Training, nd).

A project can be carried out in many ways. A guideline in the light of children's rights as outlined in the UNCRC, its principles combined with the social pedagogy theory of 'the common third' could look like this:

- *Getting started* – Team up with your colleagues for a creative methods talk, ensuring you schedule time for planning and follow-up reflections. The relational key for you and the child/children is to have fun together doing some creative work. Through this interaction, you will learn about the child's preferences and interests, and he or she will learn about you. 'When two or more people share an experience or work on a task together, something emerges that is not part of them and their mutual interrelationships. It is something outside of them, something external: I call it "the common third"' (Husen, 2022).
- *Framing the work* – Create a plan that outlines the time frame for the creative work. List the necessary equipment and organise the workflow. Ensure you have a suitable space and enough room for the activities. As much as possible, involve the child/children in the planning process. Being part of the planning, deciding on the activity or shopping for materials makes them feel involved and fosters a sense of belonging.
- *Working* – Welcome the child or children and explain what you will be doing, providing them with the necessary equipment and a short introduction talk. See yourself as a facilitator and take any initiative from the children seriously. Be open to following the child's lead. This approach is crucial for respecting the child's creativity. It also empowers the child to be an inventor in their own life. If the child gets stuck, offer immediate help. Encourage responsibility by involving them in tidying up and cleaning the workspace.

- *Exhibition* – Recognise the children's work with an exhibition. Organising an event together is very satisfying. Invite an audience and assign the children different hosting duties. If possible, provide refreshments. It would be wonderful if a child could welcome the audience, further boosting their confidence and sense of achievement.

Final comments

In this chapter, several methods and tools based on existing literature have been described. These methods are designed for professionals working with children who aim to create an environment where children can safely be heard and seen. The methods stimulate creativity and serve as helpful tools for building children's courage and action competence. Children must have the opportunity to explore and develop their communication skills in joyful and creative surroundings so that they better can make suggestions and decisions that will benefit them in the future. The report prepared by the PANDA project on methods and tools for collaborative work with young children, and its subsequent publication (Juul et al, 2023), documents additional methods and tools that further promote collaborative work with children.

Notes

[1] A comprehensive list of videos, resources and publications can be found at: Dr. Margaret Lowenfeld Trust. The World Technique (https://lowenfeld.org/the-world-technique/) and Transpersonal Sand Play Centre (http://sandplay.net/).

[2] Some recommendations based on his work that can help practitioners in their professional practice can be found on the Reacch website (see https://reacch.eu/media-library/).

References

Ahlcrona, M.F. (2012) 'The puppet's communicative potential as a mediating tool in preschool education', *International Journal of Early Childhood*, 44(2): 171–184.

Belfiore, C. (2013) 'Puppets talk children listen: How puppets are effective teaching aids for kids', *Teach*: 9–11.

Bieleninik, L., Geretsegger, M., Mössler, K., Assmus, J., Thompson, G., Gattino, G., et al (2017) 'Effects of improvisational music therapy vs enhanced standard care on symptom severity among children with autism spectrum disorder: The TIME-A randomized clinical trial', *JAMA*, 318(6): 525–535.

Boal, A. (2002) *Games for Actors and Non-actors*, London: Routledge.

Bosgraaf, L., Spreen, M., Pattiselanno, K. and van Hooren, S. (2020). 'Art therapy for psychosocial problems in children and adolescents: A systematic narrative review on art therapeutic means and forms of expression, therapist behavior, and supposed mechanisms of change', *Frontiers in Psychology*, 11. https://doi.org/10.3389/fpsyg.2020.584685

Brechet, C., d'Audigier, L. and Audras-Torrent, L. (2020) 'The use of drawing as an emotion regulation technique with children', *Psychology of Aesthetics, Creativity, and the Arts*. Available at: https://www.researchgate.net/publication/342546497_The_use_of_drawing_as_an_emotion_regulation_technique_with_children (accessed 19 May 2025).

Bratton, S.C., Ray, D., Rhine, T. and Jones, L. (2005) 'The efficacy of play therapy with children: A meta-analytic review of treatment outcomes', *Professional Psychology: Research and Practice*, 36(4): 376–390.

Butschi, C. and Hedderich, I. (2021) 'How to involve young children in a photovoice project: Experiences and results', *Forum: Qualitative Social Research*, 22(1). https://doi.org/10.17169/fqs-22.1.3457

Case, C. and Dalley, T. (1990) *Working with Children in Art Therapy*, London: Routledge.

Case, C., Dalley, T. and Reddick, D. (2023) *The Handbook of Art Therapy*, 4th edn, Abingdon: Routledge.

Clark, A. (2005) 'Ways of seeing: Using the Mosaic approach to listen to young children's perspective', in A. Clark, A.T. Kjørholt and P. Moss (eds) *Beyond listening: Children's Perspectives on Early Childhood Services*, Bristol: Policy Press, pp 29–49.

Clark, A., Moss, P. and National Children's Bureau (2011) *Listening to Young Children: The Mosaic Approach*, 2nd edn, London: National Children's Bureau.

Coholic, D., Eys, M. and Lougheed, S. (2012) 'Investigating the effectiveness of an arts-based and mindfulness-based group program for the improvement of resilience in children in need', *Journal of Child and Family Studies*, 21(5): 833–844.

Collins, F.M. and Cooper, P.J. (1997) *The Power of Story: Teaching through Storytelling*, Boston: Allyn & Bacon.

Corbett, B.A., Key, A.P., Qualls, L., Fecteau, S., Newsom, C., Coke, C. and Yoder, P. (2016) 'Improvement in social competence using a randomized trial of a theatre intervention for children with autism spectrum disorder', *Journal of Autism and Developmental Disorders*, 46(2): 658–672. https://doi.org/10.1007/s10803-015-2600-9

Dale, M. and Wagner, W. (2003) 'Sandplay: An investigation into child's meaning system via the self-confrontation method for children', *Journal of Constructive Psychology*, 16: 17–36. https://doi.org/10.1080/10720530390117849

Geretsegger, M., Elefant, C., Mössler, K.A. and Gold, C. (2014) 'Music therapy for people with autism spectrum disorder', *Cochrane Database of Systematic Reviews*, 6: CD004381. https://doi.org/10.1002/14651858.CD004381.pub3

Glew, S.G., Simonds, L.M. and Williams E.I. (2021) 'The effects of group singing on the wellbeing and psychosocial outcomes of children and young people: A systematic integrative review'. *Arts Health*, 13(3): 240–262. https://doi.org/10.1080/17533015.2020.1802604

Goldberg, M. (2017) 'Arts integration: Teaching subject matter through the arts in multicultural settings'. *Journal of Educational Research*, 110(1): 1–12. https://doi.org/10.1080/00220671.2015.1126672

Grant, D. (2017) 'Feeling for meaning: The making and understanding of image theatre'. *Research in Drama Education: The Journal of Applied Theatre and Performance*, 22(2): 186–201. https://doi.org/10.1080/13569783.2017.1286977

Hong, G.L. (2010) *Sandplay Therapy: Research and Practice*, Hoboken: Taylor & Francis.

Husen, M. (2022) 'The common third'. Available at: https://michaelhusen.dk/the-common-third/ (accessed 19 May 2025).

Isbell, R., Sobol, J., Lindauer, L. and Lowrance, A. (2004) 'The effects of storytelling and story reading on the oral language complexity and story comprehension of young children', *Early Childhood Education Journal*, 32(3): 157–163.

Johnstone, K. (1987) *Impro: Improvisation and the Theatre*, London: Routledge.

Jones, P. (2007) *Drama as Therapy: Theory Practice and Research*, London: Routledge.

Jones, P. and Pimenta, S. (2020) *Storybook Manual: An Introduction to Working with Storybooks Therapeutically and Creatively*, Abingdon: Taylor & Francis.

Juul, R. et al (2023) 'Methods and tools that inform collaborative work with the young children', in *PANDA Resources Engaging and Collaborating with Children Support for Professionals in Helping Children to Find Their Voices and Access Their Participation Rights in a Collaborative Environment*. NTNU: Norwegian University of Science and Technology, pp 31–51.

Kalff, D. (2003). *Sandplay: A Psychotherapeutic Approach to the Psyche*, Bristol, CT: Temones Press.

Karaolis, O. (2023) 'Being with a puppet: Literacy through experiencing puppetry and drama with young children', *Education Sciences*, 13(3): 291. https://doi.org/10.3390/educsci13030291

Karjalainen, S. (2020) 'Joy as a practice: Performing joy in children's everyday relations in early childhood education settings', *Early Child Development and Care*: 1–12. https://doi.org/10.1080/03004430.2020.1775593

Kröger, T. and Nupponen, A.M. (2019) 'Puppet as a pedagogical tool: A literature review', *International Electronic Journal of Elementary Education*, 11(4): 393–401. https://doi.org/10.26822/iejee.2019450797

Landreth, G.L. (2012) *Play Therapy: The Art of the Relationship*, Abingdon: Routledge.

Lee, R.M. (2015) 'Creative arts therapies in the classroom: A study on drama therapy in education', *Journal of Educational Research and Innovation*, 4(1): 1–12.

Lillard, A.S. et al (2013) 'The impact of pretend play on children's development: A review of the evidence', *Psychological Bulletin*, 139(1): 1–34. https://doi.org/10.1037/a0029321

Lowenfeld, M. (1979) *The World Technique*, Boston: Allen & Unwin.

Lowenfeld, M. (1991) *Play in Childhood*, New York: Cambridge University Press.

Lowenfeld, M. (2004) *Understanding Children's Sandplay: Lowenfeld's World Technique*, Liverpool: Liverpool University Press.

Malchiodi, C.A. (2003) 'Expressive arts therapy and multimodal approaches', *International Journal of Arts Therapy*, 8(2): 69–77.

Malchiodi, C.A. (2008) *Creative Interventions with Traumatised Children*, New York: Guilford Press.

Malchiodi, C.A. (2013) *Art Therapy and Health Care*, New York: Guilford Press.

Mayer-Benarous, H., Benarous, X., Vonthron, F. and Cohen, D. (2021) 'Music therapy for children with autistic spectrum disorder and/or other neurodevelopmental disorders: A systematic review', *Frontiers in Psychiatry*, 12. https://doi.org/10.3389/fpsyt.2021.643234

Norwegian Directorate for Education and Training (nd) 'Prosjektarbeid'. Available at: https://www.udir.no/laring-og-trivsel/stottemateriell-til-rammeplanen/pedagogisk-dokumentasjon/ped-dok-didaktisk-perspektiv/prosjektarbeid/ (accessed 19 May 2025).

Oaklander, V. (2006) *Hidden Treasure: A Map to the Child's Inner Self*, London: Karnac Books.

Pearson, M., and Wilson, H. (2019) 'Sandplay therapy: A safe, creative, space for trauma recovery', *Australian Counselling Research Journal*: 20–24.

Råde, A. (2021) 'The use of puppets as a pedagogical tool for young children: A literature review', *International Research in Early Childhood Education*, 11(3): 22–40.

Ray, D.C., Armstrong, S.A., Warren, A.T. and Balkin, R.S. (2005) 'Play therapy practices among elementary school counsellors', *Professional School Counselling*, 8(4): 360–365.

Robinson, K. (2006) 'Do schools kill creativity?' *TED Talks*. Available at: https://www.ted.com/talks/ken_robinson_says_schools_kill_creativity?language=en (accessed 19 May 2025).

Roesler, C. (2019) 'Sandplay therapy: An overview of theory, applications, and evidence base', *The Arts in Psychotherapy*, 64: 84–94. https://doi.org/10.1016/j.aip.2019.04.001

Russo, M.F., Vernam, J. and Wolbert, A. (2006) 'Sandplay and storytelling: Social constructivism and cognitive development in child counselling', *The Arts in Psychotherapy*, 33(3): 229–237. https://doi.org/10.1016/j.aip.2006.02.005

Smith, P.K., and Pellegrini, A. (2013) *Psychology of Play*, Oxford: Oxford University Press.

Stiles, K.W. and Gair, M.S. (2010) 'Using drawing for emotional expression: A case study with a preschool boy', *Journal of Creativity in Mental Health*, 5(1): 71–88.

Sonter, L.J. and Jones, D.J. (2018) 'Drawing as a tool to support children's executive function in play', *International Art in Early Childhood Research Journal*, 1(1): 1–22.

Syabila, H. and Irvan, M. (2023) 'The effect of interactive hand puppet on joint attention ability in children with autism', in A.P. Wibawa et al (eds) *ICE 2022 ASSEHR 736*: 90–98. https://doi.org/10.2991/978-2-38476-020-6_10

Tan, P. (2019) 'Listening to young children: A Mosaic approach. Research perspectives from two children and dinosaurs', *SFU Educational Review*, 12(2): 64–78. https://doi.org/10.21810/sfuer.v12i2.932

Thrana, H.M., Gjeitnes, K. and Iversen, E.H. (2023) 'Painting workshop: A tool for improving communication and social interaction', *European Social Work Research*, 1(3): 312–328. https://doi.org/10.1332/ZPEA1281

United Nations (1989) *Convention on the Rights of the Child*. Treaty Series, 1577, 3. Available at: https://www.ohchr.org/en/instruments-mechanisms/instruments/convention-rights-child (accessed 19 May 2025).

Veale, A. (2005) 'Researching Children's Experiences', in S. Greene and D. Hogan (eds) *Researching Children's Experiences*, London: Sage, pp 253–273.

Wieder, S. (2017) 'The power of symbolic play in emotional development through the DIR lens', *Topics in Language Disorders*, 37(3): 259–281. https://doi.org/10.1097/TLD.0000000000000126

Williams, E., Dingle, G. A. and Clift, S. (2018) 'A systematic review of mental health and wellbeing outcomes of group singing for children and young people', *Arts & Health*, 10(1): 1–19.

SIX

Listening and talking to young children outdoors

Inger Sofie Dahlø Husby, Pål Børmark and Solvår Hernes

Introduction

Spending time outdoors is a common activity in Norway. Families, kindergartens and schools regularly take children out on hiking trips in forest and fields, by the sea and in mountains. There is a saying in Norway that everyone is born with skis attached to their legs. This means that skiing is mandatory as soon as one can walk and that for many, skiing becomes an innate skill.

Outings and activities close to nature are typical activities in residential childcare in Norway too. They vary from going away on cabin outings to short trips in the local environment (Haaland and Tønnessen, 2022). Outdoor life is regarded as a specific Norwegian cultural heritage and is a strong part of Norwegian identity (Klima- og miljødepartement, 2016). That said, the principles of engaging with children outside are not restricted to the Norwegian context and the ideas explored in this chapter are applicable to outdoor settings in countries across the globe.

In this chapter, we explore how child welfare services can use this 'outdoor room' of the natural world for conversations with children, instead of the traditional 'indoor room' of offices and interview/therapy rooms. Engaging in conversation under the sky repositions both the child and the adult as they both stand on shared, neutral ground. Together, they can enjoy seeing a bird in the sky or be annoyed by the smell after the farmer has spread manure on the ground. It is easier for both the child and the adult to be free from formal routines and bureaucratic requirements. Being outside together enables a child and an adult to get closer to each other in ways that differ from the indoor interview and/or therapy room.

The aim of this chapter is to explore the opportunities that lie in using outdoor activities and outings as a resource to unmute children's voices. We want to demonstrate the importance of an alternative to the traditional 'therapeutic room'. Our experience is that the traditional therapeutic context (the general idea of two persons in a closed room) can be a strange, awkward or even frightening experience for young children. Conversations with children require something different from the adult way of talking. Engaging in collaborative inquiry about private topics is easier when children and adults are engaged together in chosen outdoor activities in a familiar context.

Based on experience from a Norwegian child welfare day unit centre (hereinafter called 'the Centre'), we present a typical practice example of a ten-year-old girl called Ann (pseudonym) receiving support. We have developed a practice scenario based on Ann's experiences. With this child in mind and drawing on our other experiences from working with other young children, we unpack the concept of outdoor activities as an effective participatory medium for creating helping relationships and conversations. We demonstrate how the outdoor activity with Ann contributed to her lowering her guard and helped her to broach talking about difficult issues. Employing insights from social pedagogy, we seek to make sense of our experience and explore different kinds of outdoor activities. We conclude by offering some tips for keeping children safe outside and make three key recommendations for practice.

Box 6.1: Ten-year-old Ann

Ann is being assessed by the Centre. She has been increasingly absent from school in the last school year. In conversations, she has said that school is boring and that she prefers to be at home in her apartment.

Ann says that in her spare time she likes animals and drawing, and likes to watch videos on her mobile phone. She has a friend who she visits from time to time. When the social worker made a recent home visit, Ann enjoyed showing them a small box with attractive shells in it.

Ann is open to discussing her daily activities, but prefers not to divulge information regarding her personal thoughts, emotions or family matters. Ann has stated to child welfare services that she doesn't like talking to other people.

Last month, there was an incident at Ann's family home where neighbours had contacted the police due to a disturbance between the mother and her partner. The mother told the child welfare service that the event was terrifying, and she would like to continue the contact and get more support because she was concerned about her daughter's wellbeing.

During conversations with Ann, the practitioner received little response to different questions about her welfare or the circumstances relating to the last incident at home. The most common answer from Ann was 'I don't know'.

This example concerning Ann is typical of children who receive in-home support in Norway. Ann spends a lot of time at home with her mother and she visits the Centre for afternoons once or twice a week. The child's care plan has two main objectives: (i) to become familiar with the challenges Ann faces at home and at school; and (ii) to prevent further school absences and enhance her general wellbeing. There is a mutual interest among the adults, even a concern, about finding out what Ann thinks and feels, and why she acts as she does when it comes to difficulties in school or at home.

Participation through outdoor activity conversations

Ann has the right to be involved in her own case and to have a say. However, like many other children in contact with child welfare services, Ann does not talk easily about close relationships and the conditions at home (Clifford et al, 2015). These feelings are common to many children involved in child welfare services who have little trust in adults, are often on their guard and tend to be reticent about sharing information (Juul and Husby, 2020, Tait and Wosu, 2013). Winter et al (2017) refer to similar findings, in that some of the children resisted contact with social workers. In this study, some of the children experienced their social worker negatively as a threat to their relationships with their family. In addition, research shows that children's voices are not taken seriously in child welfare decision-making processes (Winter, 2011; McCafferty and Mercado Garcia, 2023), and this further erodes children's trust in social workers.

Children identify trusting relationships as essential if they are going to open up in conversations with social workers (Salkauskiene et al, 2023). Given this knowledge, it is crucial that such relationships are enabled in order to respect the right of children to express their views and for their views to be given due weight (UNCRC, 1989, Article 12). In the case of Ann, she has challenges at home and at school. The information so far indicates that Ann feels unsafe and/or disconnected in both arenas. There is a need for changes that ensure Ann has a safer upbringing, where she learns, develops and experiences safety, love and care from her mother and other people close to her. To make this happen in a way that make sense to ten-year-old Ann, her social worker requires knowledge of her experiences, feelings, wishes and capability. Staying close to the law and Article 12 UNCRC, it is relevant to ask the following question: how does Ann view the life situation she is currently experiencing?

According to Warming (2011), there is a difference between children's own articulated perspectives and the adults' attempts to understand a child's situation. Ann's own lived experiences of her family and the other adults and children she socialises with is different from outsider adults' perspectives. In helping processes with children like Ann, respecting both perspectives is necessary. Framing the process as an exploratory collaboration makes it possible to appreciate both viewpoints, as we become co-subjects who seek common understanding and recognise another's standpoint as enriching of the understanding. From this perspective, it moves from positioning the relationships as a competition about who holds the truth and 'is right' (Aasland, 2014). Warming (2011) argues that adult helpers cannot act in a competent manner without knowing the child's own view. Conversations are the tool to get to know and understand more of children's own perspectives on their lives. However, since we are adults, we can never see the world completely as children see it, but if we strive and listen carefully, we can get closer to children's everyday lived experiences (Arner and Tellgren, 2011; Warming, 2011).

Ann is assumed to have experiences and feelings which the adults need to know about in order to be of support and to help her in the best possible way. Consequently, for Ann, conversations with an adult or a social worker are important. So far, Ann has not said anything about the incident at home when the police came to the door, nor has she expressed details about the conditions at school. The case scenario regarding Ann is further developed in Box 6.2 in order to explore how engaging in outdoor activities can facilitate meaningful conversations between her and the social worker.

Box 6.2: Engaging Ann in outdoor activities to facilitate communication

In Norway, everyone has access to the shore and the beach, all year round. At low tide, there are crabs, hermit crabs and other small sea creatures to be found. There are also shells in various sizes and snail shells. It is only a short walk from the Centre to the shore. The social worker, Inge, has extensive experience with children and excursions outdoors. Since Ann has a collection of shells at home, Inge wants to invite Ann on a shell treasure hunt to look for snail shells, mussel shells and so on. Ann has also shown an interest in animals. In case Ann becomes bored of looking for shells, this activity can easily be combined with looking for crabs and other creepy-crawlies.

In planning this outdoor activity, Inge starts by asking Ann to bring her collection of shells the next time she shows up. Ann responds positively to the request. Next time, she brings the box and proudly shows off the different shell types. Inge introduces the idea of a trip to the shore to look for shells and suggests that together they make a new collection for the Centre. Ann gets very excited about this suggestion. She is immediately happy and wants to go out. Inge says they need to prepare by organising their boots for the next time they meet and gathering buckets and spades from the Centre. Dinner will soon be ready and while they wait Inge suggests that Ann find pictures of shells on her mobile phone and makes a drawing of the different varieties. Ann likes the idea of drawing seashells and gets down to business straight away. Inge also takes part in drawing, and they fill in a large sheet of shells and snail shells. Along the way, they talk back and forth about the name of the shells and Ann also says that she stayed home from school today as she had felt a little unwell.

The following Wednesday afternoon, when there was low tide, Inge brings hot chocolate in a thermos and a couple of slices of bread, buckets and spades, and she and Ann set off with their boots on. It's a sunny day; both are happy to go out for a walk. Ann tells Inge that she has been home from school again today. She expresses that she has been so excited all week about the outing and that she had to sleep this morning to be ready for the shell hunt. It is the big spring this day, and there are shells everywhere. The buckets fill up quickly. They have plenty of time and they wash the shells and lay them out to dry in the sun. Inge takes out the thermos and pours a cup for each of them, while they sit next to each other, partly looking at the 'catch', partly looking out to sea and the tide that rises slowly. Inge begins in an open and friendly mode: 'You know one thing, lately I've been thinking a lot about how you experience everyday life at home with mum. Your teacher has also called me and says she misses you at school.' Ann falls silent, both look out over the sea, and no one says anything for several minutes. The sun has started to set and it has become completely windless. Ann begins in a low voice: 'I don't know what I can say. Mum says that I must say as little as possible to you, since you can take me away from her and I must live with other parents, in a foster home or something.' The conversation goes back and forth, and together they explore the tasks that the child protection service is set to do in

Norway. They end the conversation and Ann summarises it this way: 'When I get home, I'll tell mum that a child protection worker is more like a teacher, when children get the wrong answer to the calculations, the child welfare professionals teach them how to get it right. They are not like the police who punish people when someone breaks the rules or makes a mistake.'

Examining this scenario through the lens of social pedagogical theory can generate significant insights and better prepare social workers to use outdoor excursions to effectively engage in conversations about difficult and upsetting subjects with young children. Social pedagogy puts everyday activities, dialogues and relationships between child and the adult at the forefront (Eichsteller and Holthoff, 2011; Petrie, 2011a, 2011b), and the unique significance of these three elements in Ann's situation are explored in the following text.

Social pedagogical principles and practice

Activities

Within social pedagogical thinking, activities such as having a meal, doing homework, and playing indoors and outdoors are seen as meaningful pedagogical activities that promote participation, interpersonal support, learning and identity development. As the pedagogues and the children are engaged in the same task, these activities constitute what is referred to as 'the common third' – that is, a third party in their interaction (Petrie, 2011a, p 79). In the storyline mentioned earlier, Ann is invited on a shell hunt activity at the shore. It is a shared task, joy and effort. The shell collection can create happiness for the others at the Centre, the shells are pretty to look at, they can be used to make decorations and small gifts to give away, and everyone (both adults and children at the Centre) can learn more about different types of sea and snail shells (see Figure 6.1). However, beyond learning,

Figure 6.1: Decoration

Source: Photo by Inger Sofie Dahlø Husby

knowledge and everyday happiness, joint activities in social pedagogy nurture the adult–child relationships and create space for dialogue (Petrie, 2011b). Ann's voice is unmuted. In dialogue with the social worker, Inge, Ann challenges her fears and allows herself to be informed about how child welfare services assist families.

Dialogue

Social pedagogy is a dialogic practice. The professional does not act as a teacher or a therapist; rather, they work alongside others as 'social pedagogues see themselves as sharing the same "living space" as the people they work with' (Petrie, 2011b, 9). The work is done through dialogue, in the belief that different perspectives add to the richness and creativity. Gradovski (2018), informed by Bakthin (1986), suggests that the dialogue in social pedagogy is important in its own right. In conversations, we mutually influence each other; whether we agree or disagree and in a wider sense, our whole life is a dialogue with the world around us – we are influenced and we ourselves influence each other. However, with this agency comes responsibility and the opportunity to influence the power relationships into which we enter. This takes on the following meaning in the case of Ann. Ann's views and experiences become important, as individuals are experts in their own lives. Individuals construct their own reality in accordance with their subjective experiences (Eichsteller and Holthoff, 2011). Together with information from her mother, her teacher and other adults, Ann's experiences add necessary details to make up the 'picture' of her situation, illustrating how different perspectives contribute to the everyday richness of experience.

Up until now, Ann had been at a loss for words and just answered 'I don't know', 'school is boring' and so on. Why is that? In the story mentioned earlier, we learn that Ann is holding back for fear that something 'worse' might happen to her and her family; child welfare services may take her away from her mother. Ann takes on the responsibility of keeping the family together. She can withstand all the questioning from the social worker. However, in this outdoor activity conversation with a dialogic, caring and trusting social worker, she (figuratively speaking) opens the door. It turns out that she needs to find out more about how child welfare services assist families. The conversation has clearly made a difference to both individuals involved. Ann has gained a more enlightened and nuanced view of the child welfare service tasks and Inge has gained insight to better understand why Ann holds back. Ann is ready for the next step, which involves enlisting her mother's help with the supportive, not punitive, guidance of child welfare services.

Relationships

Through a socio-pedagogical lens, joint activities like this outing are seen as an opportunity to build trusting relationships. The connection is seen as equal in the sense of equal dignity as human beings, but the relationship is not equal in terms of ability. Inge is clearly more 'powerful' than the child; however, this disparity must be used in the best interests of the child (Bjørknes, 2018). Eichsteller and Holthoff (2011, p 44) frame the question of power imbalance like this: 'power is used not as a form of control but as responsibility, a relationship that leads to less dependence on the social pedagogue and facilitates a person's increasing ability to access resources themselves'.

On the other hand, this power imbalance does not mean that children are without 'power'. As the social pedagogical approach endorses children's agency (Eichsteller and Holthoff, 2011), children are not considered to be powerless in social relations and conversations; they are recognised as agentic and very able to exercise power in meetings with adults. Their voices influence the interaction, and they can also resist and oppose input from adults. The ethical dilemma arises in determining the extent of power that should be granted to the child. In the scenario with Ann, this means that Inge has a particular responsibility to ensure that Ann's perspectives (experiences) are known among the staff, respected and given proper consideration in the Centre's planning process.

Various forms of outdoor activities

Start exploring together

The number of outdoor activities where young children can participate is only limited by our creativity. The relational stance that leads to exploring experiences and activities with children is crucial. Young people have skills and knowledge. As adults, we can support that by invitations and curiosity, questions and suggestions. Children are the experts in knowing what they like to do, what kind of activities they prefer to engage in, what they yet have not tried, what they are curious about or fun activities they have heard other children describe. As adults, we can choose how we position, talk or act in relation to children. Searching for competence, experience, knowledge or joy is a relational stance which can be recognised and understood by young children. Children like to contribute when they are invited to do so.

Ask children themselves

Based on our experiences from the Centre and our experiences from other child welfare work, we have learned that children know a lot about their everyday life and many like to share their expert knowledge or educate adults in their practical field of experiences. Steer conversations with children towards topics that energise them and foster their passion and involvement, asking questions like the following:

- The last time you had fun, what did you do?
- Who was with you in that moment?
- How did that idea come up?

Fun is a highly valued and indispensable activity for children. It is important to be interested in what children and parents find enjoyable. Ask children, parents, colleagues and also check out social media to find out the following:

- What activities, interests and experiences do the children or the child's network talk about? Be active in exploring or asking about experiences, interests and topics that children like or know about in their local environment
- Ask children and families about the activities and places within easy reach in their local area
- What do colleagues know about from local/social media regarding what is happening in your local environment?
- What takes place outdoors locally – what free activities, events and gatherings are coming up or in action?

Think small

A common obstacle is the financial aspect, since participating in certain activities with children may involve financial expenditure. However, many different types of activities can be carried out in a reasonable and sustainable way – think small. Overall, many popular activities and places that children know are typically associated with low costs.

Engaging the children in a treasure hunt in the neighbourhood can give a very different focus compared to earlier walks in well-known streets, parks, beaches and shores. You may look out for branches, leaves or cones from a tree, shells, snail shells, waste, lost items or plastic from people who spent time in the same park, and turn these items into ornaments, decorative objects (as seen earlier in Figure 6.1) or artwork later on.

Bring indoors activities outside

A lot of indoor activities like boardgames, puzzles, drawing and water painting, reading and listening to music can be brought outside if the weather is on your side. To share a meal or eat some fruit or snacks is an activity familiar to many children. Drinking hot chocolate, tea, or coffee feels

Figure 6.2: Two boys on an outdoor walk

Source: Photo by Inger Sofie Dahlø

even nicer when you are outside, like on a bench or sitting on the grass or in the forest on a winter's day. The very same grass can easily be transformed into a frisbee field, badminton court or football pitch. Younger children can inspire themselves in new surroundings by connecting with their imagination and their skills and talents. By pointing out, asking the children or commenting on something, creativity can arise: 'a tree can be a castle, or a log can be a horse'. Remember, transportable, light and low-cost equipment is often the very best.

A photo outing

A trip can be turned into an 'expedition' when children bring along a smartphone or a camera and take pictures of interesting objects or places.

The animal kingdom

Animals are very popular to be around. A dog can turn a walk into something completely different. Having access to different types of animals is not always easy, but there are often a lot of dogs, cats or even horses around where people live. Some animals can be visited or even borrowed for a walk. In the case of Ann, she began to talk enthusiastically about Bob when she was asked about friends or those she liked being around. It turned out that Bob was a terrier, a seven-year-old dog living in the same street. With the permission of the owner, Bob gladly joined us for a walk on one of the following days.

Outdoors safety

As described previously, many Norwegian people have a fondness of the outdoors and using nature for recreation. By experiencing nature, you also become aware of risks when moving around outdoors. Children are taught of these risks from an early age. In Norway, most children are familiar with nearby nature through their families or through the education system. Kindergartens and schools use the outdoors as a part of teaching, and children are exposed to the shifting weather, getting wet, freezing, sweating, creating a bonfire, hiking, eating outdoors and exploring the Norwegian wildlife (see Figure 6.2). They get to climb trees, run, jump, swim and so on. At our Centre, we build on these experiences and want the children we meet to appreciate nature and motivate them to use their surroundings to cope with the difficulties they are experiencing.

Even though we stress the fact that it is mostly safe to use the shore, the woods, the lakes and the mountains, we have to make sure the settings are safe and secure for the children when we use the outdoors for therapeutic purposes. This means we must create settings where children feel emotionally and physically safe.

To make the settings and activities attractive for the children, and somewhere that they can feel emotionally secure, we do some preparations. The children, young adults or families who attend our outdoor groups or individual meetings have different needs. We communicate, therefore, with each of them in advance to ensure their needs or concerns can be satisfactorily addressed. The issues we address might be where exactly we are going, what we are going to do, what they would like to do, who will attend, how we will get there, how long we will stay, who except our group may be at the same place and so on. For some children and young adults, they find safety in bringing a friend. Sometimes their mobile phone is what gives them the sense of safety.

At the Centre, we choose to be open to most suggestions in order to create a safe setting, which in turn can lead to a therapeutic setting. We have many experiences where knowing they can withdraw at any point enables children and adolescents to feel safe. They know that at any given time, they have the possibility to go back, be driven home, call someone or just stop the activity. If we are on a trip out of town for the activity or on overnight activity trips, there are always enough social workers present to bring a child back home if the setting is experienced as unsafe. Just knowing that there is the option to leave can give a sense of safety.

The other type of safety to have in mind is creating settings where everyone involved is physically safe. We must take safety precautions, which means checking out what possible dangers are in the surroundings, what the weather forecast says, making sure we have the right equipment for this kind of activity, have a first aid kit in handy, bring a phone with a charged battery and have plenty of food and drinks. The social workers need to have knowledge about the activity or make agreements with companies that have the expected knowledge and safety measures to lead the activity. Examples of these kinds of activities that we sometimes use are dog sledding, horseriding, fishing trips in boats and canoeing,

Sometimes feeling emotionally safe and physically safe are two aspects to safety that are hard to separate. Safety precautions might be in place, but the child still might feel unsafe in the activity. This is usually attributable to a child lacking experience of knowing whether they will be able to achieve the tasks that are ahead of them, whether this involves starting a bonfire or taking a leap on a zipline. These situations are particularly good therapeutic sessions because they give us an opportunity to sensitively challenge the child about their emotional responses and capabilities. In our experience, children will very often have positive emotions after managing things they did not think (or know) they were able to do.

In Ann's example, there are not a lot of physical safety precautions that need to be in place for collecting shells, but on an emotional level, it is crucial that she is well informed about what's going to happen as part of the outdoor activity, who will attend and where they are going. The fact that they are collecting shells might make it safe because we know she likes to collect shells and she gets to show them to other children at the Centre, since the plan is to keep them there. The trip to the shoreline is near the Centre's location so they will not have to travel, and she will be able to go back at any time.

Parents are always informed of activities in which their children take part, and they have given permission for the Centre to let their children participate. To make sure everyone is safe in the outdoor activities, we must adapt the activity to children's maturity level and age. Furthermore, we must assess the actual context and its risk factors, adjusting the activity, the number of participants and the number of social workers present to consider the safety measures mentioned earlier.

Closing thoughts

We recommend outdoor, activity-based conversations since children can feel more comfortable sharing their thoughts and feelings in such an environment. Given the variety of nature-based activities that could be taken up, we recommend starting with asking the children themselves what they like to do outdoors. We concurrently advocate for low-expense outdoor activities. Importantly, when it comes to children's safety on trips outside, it is vital to remain aware that a child may feel physically, but not necessarily emotionally, safe. That said, our experience has shown us that moving outside into nature is a stress-relieving activity for both children and adults, and we have seen how such opportunities enable us all to become more receptive to each other's input, and that undoubtedly is a good outcome.

References

Arner, E. and Tellgren, B. (2011) Ba*rns syn på vuxna – att komma nåra barns perspektiv*, Lund: Studentlitteratur AB.

Aasland, D.G. (2014) 'Hvem er vi? Om samarbeidets subjekt', in H.H. Grelland et al (eds) *Samarbeidets filosofi*, Oslo: Gyldendal Akademisk, pp 19–37.

Bjørknes, L.E. (2018) 'Protect human dignity', in L.E. Bjørknes et al (ed) *Sosialpedagogikkens mangfold*, Bergen: Fagbokforlaget, pp 95–111.

Clifford, G. et al (2015) *Minst hjelp til dem som trenger det mest? Sluttrapport fra forsknings- og utviklingsprosjektet 'Det nye barnevernet'*, Bodø: Nordlandsforskning.

Eichsteller, G. and Holthoff, S. (2011) 'Conceptual foundations of social pedagogy: A transnational perspective from Germany', in C. Cameron and P. Moss (eds) *Social Pedagogy and Working with Children and Young People: Where Care and Education Meet*, London: Jessica Kingsley, pp 33–52.

Gradovski, M. (2018) 'Min forståelse av dialogens rolle i sosialpedagogisk praksis', L.E. Bjørknes et al (eds) *Sosialpedagogikkens mangfold*, Bergen: Fagbokforlaget, pp 155–160.

Haaland, J.J. and Tønnessen, M. (2022) 'Recreation in the outdoors: exploring the experience of adolescents in residential care', *Child & Youth Services*, 43(3): 206–308. https://doi.org/10.1080/0145935X.2022.2044771

Juul, R. and Husby, I.S.D. (2020) 'Collaboration and conversations with children in child welfare services: Parents' viewpoint', *Child and Family Social Work*, 25(S1): 9–17. https://doi.org/10.1111/cfs.12707

Klima- og miljødepartement (2016) *Frilufsliv – Natur som kilde til helse og livskvalitet. Stortingsmelding No. 18 (2015–2016)*. Available at: https://www.regjeringen.no/contentassets/9147361515a74ec8822c8dac5f43a95a/no/pdfs/stm201520160018000dddpdfs.pdf (accessed 19 May 2025).

McCafferty, P. and Mercado Garcia, E. (2023) 'Children's participation in child welfare: A systematic review of systematic reviews', *British Journal of Social Work*, 54(3): 1092–1108. https://doi.org/10.1093/bjsw/bcad167

Petrie, P. (2011a) 'Interpersonal communication: The medium for social pedagogic practice', in C. Cameron and P. Moss (eds) *Social Pedagogy and Working with Children and Young People: Where Care and Education Meet*, London: Jessica Kingsley, pp 69–83.

Petrie, P. (2011b) *Communication Skills for Working with Children and Young People: Introducing Social Pedagogy*, London: Jessica Kingsley.

Salkauskiene, I., Wilson, S., Gresdahl, M. and Juul, R. (2023) 'Children's experiences of collaborative relationship with child welfare and protection professionals in Norway: a state-of-the-art review', *Nordic Social Work Research*: 1–17. https://doi.org/10.1080/2156857X.2023.2298673

Tait, A. and Wosu, H. (2013) *Direct Work with Vulnerable Chidren: Playful Activities and Strategies for Communication*, London: Jessica Kingsley.

UNCRC (United Nations Convention on the Rights of the Child) (1989) *United Nations Convention on the Rights of the Child*, Geneva: United Nations.

Warming, H. (2011) *Børneperspektiver: børn som ligeværdige medspillere i socialt og pædagogisk arbejde*, Copenhagen: Akademisk forlag.

Winter, K. (2011) *Building Relationships and Communciating with Young Children: A Practial Guide for Social Workers*, Abingdon: Routledge.

Winter, K. et al (2017) 'Exploring communication between social workers, children and young people', *British Journal of Social Work*, 47(5): 1427–1444. https://doi.org/10.1093/bjsw/bcw083

SEVEN

Key principles in participation and collaboration with young children

Karen Winter and Gillian Ruch

Introduction

This book has drawn together the combined frameworks, approaches, practices and resources that underpin the participation rights of young children in professional practice in child welfare and child protection. We have been struck by our deep, shared commitment to practice in this area, which has been shaped and informed by significant and substantial professional experience over many years and often in challenging circumstances. We have been encouraged by our shared principles which underpin our work and that are grounded in the United Nations Convention on the Rights of the Child (UNCRC). We have also been surprised about the ongoing gaps, especially in relation to the implementation of the participation rights of the very youngest of our children, including our babies and our infants. We are encouraged to hear of recent developments, including findings from research by Heirbaut and Eerdekens (2023) and policy developments in Scotland where the 'Voice of the Infant: Best Practice Guidelines and an Infant Pledge' were published by the Scottish government in 2023. We begin this chapter with an overview of our journey and then reflect on the principles of practice which we hope provide optimism, strength, support and confidence in taking practice forward in this area.

An overview of our journey

We started in Chapter 1 with an overview of the PANDA project and its intentional design to link theory and practice through the mixture of representatives – academics and practitioners – in the PANDA team. In focusing on children's rights in Chapter 2, we sought to underline their importance as the cornerstone for everything we do in our work with young children and acknowledged them to be the core foundation of, and the golden thread that runs through, all that is written about in the subsequent chapters. By way of contrast, the specificity of participatory practices in individual nations is outlined in Chapter 3. This chapter highlighted the context specific nature of participatory practices with young children, which are dependent on social, economic, political, cultural and legislative structures in each of the four PANDA project countries. Chapter 4 explored how very young children, babies and infants' participation is facilitated through attuned and attentive professional practice. The chapter illustrated how a young child can be included in conversations and how adults can improve practice by being attuned to and aligned with the communicative capacity of each child. In Chapter 5, a wider range of creative methods with young children was outlined, introducing different opportunities for ensuring that very young children are heard and that their views are considered. Chapter 6 took us into the outdoors, a space in which relating with children often happens in Norway, but is less visible in the three other PANDA project countries. In this chapter, we reflected on what we have learnt and highlighted the key messages for child welfare professionals and children.

Moving forwards

Overall, this book provides rich possibilities for participatory practices with babies, infants and young children, founded on shared UNCRC-informed principles and introduced in context-specific ways to reflect the policy and legislative structures of individual countries. The UNCRC principles, outlined in General Comment No. 12: The Right of the Child to Be Heard (CRC, 2009, para 134, p 29), state that participatory practices must embed the following characteristics: be open and informative, voluntary, based on respect, relevant, child-friendly, inclusive, supported by training, safe and sensitive to risk, and accountable. Participatory practices must also be premised on an acceptance that the participation rights of every child, regardless of age, should be respected, as is noted in the following text:

> The Committee wishes to emphasise that article 12 applies both to younger and to older children. As holders of rights, even the youngest children are entitled to express their views, which should be 'given due weight in accordance with the age and maturity of the child' (art. 12.1). Young children are acutely sensitive to their surroundings and very rapidly acquire understanding of the people, places and routines in their lives, along with awareness of their own unique identity. They make choices and communicate their feelings, ideas and wishes in numerous ways, long before they are able to communicate through the conventions of spoken or written language. (CRC, 2009, para 14, p 7)

Thus, there is an obligation on individuals, teams, organisations and governments to enact the participation rights of young children. Responsibility for progress rests across professionals at all levels: governmental, managerial and individual.

Individual professionals and participatory principles in practice

To address the challenge outlined in General Comment No. 7 and to implement participatory practice requires that practitioners place children at the heart of their practice and start from the child's perspective. How would it feel for a young child to meet me? What does the space we meet in feel like, smell like and sound like to a child? How could I and the space be more child-friendly so that I can listen to a very young child? To genuinely listen to and understand young children requires professionals to adopt an open-minded disposition which is both a skill and an attitude. Child-centred professionals recognise the important and sensitive nature of the work that they do, but at the same time are aware that building trusting and respectful relationships with young children also needs to be practical, playful and fun. The strapline for Kitbag (https://www.iffkitbag.com), a resource for promoting children's emotional and social literacy, is 'Kitbag is a playful resource for serious work', a sentiment we place at the heart of participatory practice.

Participatory professionals are prepared to be courageous and take risks to ensure their practice maximises children's potential to participate. Professionals may be required to do something they do not feel confident in doing – for example, engaging in an outdoor activity or art-based creative method. They need to be comfortable with the child being the leader/ teacher/expert. Being open and informative is fundamental to participatory practice and requires professionals to be willing to hand over some of the control and their power to children. Participatory practices require a willingness among professionals to slow down and go at the pace of the child. It also requires an ability to sit with 'uncertainty' and 'not knowing', willing to trust the process that something can (and will) emerge in its own timeframes. A mind-minded attitude involves careful and slow noticing and observing, and the thoughtful formulation of hypotheses. Such hypotheses should always adopt a 'not-knowing' position and 'sit lightly' in relation to adult knowledge and power.

Participatory professionals are willing to be collaborative and vulnerable to not knowing the answer, seeking guidance from the child, advice from the parents or different perspectives and expertise from other professionals. As the well-known African proverb says, 'it takes a village to raise a child', and in the context of child welfare, this refers to the diverse network of professionals involved in any one child's life and the vital importance of them working collaboratively in the best interests of that child. When professional differences or power hierarchies are at risk of dominating the work of the group, everyone involved needs to take a pause and note that the paramountcy of the child's welfare needs to be repositioned at the centre of their multidisciplinary work together. As our Spanish colleagues working with children from the marginalised Roma community reminded us, it is vital for children's participation to be real and not simply rhetoric. It must be experienced through a participatory process and this learning process is the route to full and meaningful citizenship. Participation is a right that is reflected in a participatory attitude – 'relational participation', which leads to connectedness and is contextual, involving parents, other family members and professional colleagues.

Managers and participatory principles in practice

Managers committed to this collaborative way of working are required to provide appropriate supervisory support at the individual and collective levels. Individual and group supervision provide ideal spaces for professionals to share the emotional challenges and demands of the work. Managers may be required to advocate for staff time to be protected and for organisational and structural barriers that affect participatory practice (lack of time, lack of financial and practical resources, lack of training and lack of attention to young children's rights in practice guidelines and assessment forms) to be addressed. They may also be required to establish reflective spaces in which professionals have time to explore the contextual, relational and nuanced aspects of participatory practice and to reflect on their own values and develop their skills and knowledge. Managers may also be required to advocate for their colleagues to receive continuous professional development. Such developmental opportunities might address areas such as: child development; the impact of trauma on a child's emotional/psychological wellbeing and communicative experiences and capacities; very young children's capacities, including how babies and infants communicate their needs in complex ways through their body movements, gestures, noises and eyes; and the emotional impact on workers when engaging in such work.

Policy makers and participatory principles in practice

We believe that the full incorporation of the UNCRC into domestic law (as is evident in this project in Norway, for example, and has recently occurred in Scotland) is a priority. We acknowledge that the political, economic, cultural and social contexts of different countries create enablers and challenges, and that the UNCRC is not without critique as a Westernised human rights framework. That said, we also recognise that the adoption of the UNCRC by so many different countries offers the best potential to protect and promote the rights of all children and to address gaps in the participation rights of our youngest children. Having had the opportunity to visit other countries, to learn from each other and to identify factors that act as forces for positive change, we can see the influence of the UNCRC on participatory practice in differing contexts.

We also believe that policy makers should engage in training on the participation rights of babies, infants and young children, and ensure that they make training opportunities available for their teams. On our website (https://reacch.eu), there is a wide range of resources gathered from our different countries and contexts, freely available for all professionals to facilitate the development of values, skills and knowledge. These include research briefs (on theories, methods, communicative processes and challenges) vimeos (demonstrating practice in action), management and policy guidelines (to be used to assess the strengths and gaps and organisational and policy levels) and a training package (comprising four mini-modules). All resources are freely available, and the training package could be disseminated, adapted and accredited in country-specific contexts to facilitate the development of values, skills and knowledge in this area. We hope that colleagues (students, practitioners from differing backgrounds, managers and policy makers) will be inspired by the richness and diversity of resources, which highlight the possibilities and opportunities for enhancing participatory practices with young children. We also hope that engagement with these varied resources leads to structural and individual improvements to safeguard and promote the rights of babies, infants and very young children.

References

CRC (Committee on the Rights of the Child) (2009) *General Comment No. 12: The Right of the Child to Be Heard*, Geneva: United Nations.

Heirbaut, E. and Eerdekens, W. (2025) 'Participatie van infants in de jeugdhulp', research report. Ghent: Artevelde University of Applied Sciences.

United Nations (1989) *Convention on the Rights of the Child*, Geneva: United Nations.

Index

References to figures appear in *italic* type;
those in **bold** type refer to tables.

A

active citizenship 44–45, 46, 121
age discrimination 21
agency 21–22, 22–23, 57, 106, 107
art-based creative approaches 74, 86–88, *87*, *88*, **89**, 120
articles of UNCRC *see specific articles (for example, UNCRC Article 12)*
assessments 62–64
attitudes *see* participatory attitudes/mindsets

B

babies
  assessments and 62–64
  behaviours 56, 57–58, 63
  mentalisation and 57–59, 60
  observations of 61–62
  participation rights 56–57
  the term 'baby' 56
  see also best interests of children; capacities; communication; participation rights; rights; views of children; voices of children
behaviour 56, 57–58, 63

Belgium (Flanders)
  author's overview of 34
  child welfare challenges in 37–38
  child welfare services in 34–35
  PANDA project team 5, **6**, 7
  participation of children in 36–37
  UNCRC and 34
  very young children 55
best interests of children
  paramount, as 63, 121
  parental responsibilities 39
  power imbalances and 107
  UNCRC/General Comments and 17, *18*, 20, 28–29
  views of children and 28–29, 49
Boal, Augusto 83

C

capacities
  assessment of 24–25
  parents, of 27
  presumption of 24
  support needs, and 41–42
  UNCRC/General Comments and 18, *19*, 20, 23–25, 26–27
  very young children, of 57–59, 67–68, 122

INDEX

young children, of 21–22, 23–25, **30**, 41–42
caregivers *see* parents/caregivers
Case, C. 86
case studies 100–104, 105, 106–107
Child Welfare Act (Norway) 48, 49
child welfare/protection
  assessments 62–64
  Belgium (Flanders) 34–35, 37–38
  Northern Ireland 38–40, 42–43
  Norway 47–48, 50
  observations 61–62
  parental support 64
  Spain 46
  see also outdoor settings; professionals; social workers
children
  agency 21–22, 22–23, 57, 107
  case studies 100–104, 105, 106–107
  trusting relationships with, building 71, 101, 106, 107, 120
  see also babies; best interests of children; capacities; communication; infants; participation rights; very young children; views of children; voices of children
Children Order (Northern Ireland) 39
Children's Ombudsman Act (Norway) 49–50
citizenship 44–45, 46, 121
Clark, A. 82
Committee on the Rights of the Child (CRC) 2, 17, 19
common third 79, 90, 104
communication
  behaviour as 56, 57–58, 63
  disabilities, children with 26
  nonverbal 21, 25–26, 28, 49, 63, 73, 86
  professionals with young children 4, 65, **67**
  resources 9

  rights 48–49
  supporting of 41–42
  UNCRC on 21–22, 119
  very young children, of 21, 23, 56, 65, 122
  see also creative approaches; outdoor settings
competence of children 36, 64, 91
complaints 36, 37, 40
consent 36, 40, 48
context 12, 22, 27 *see also* Belgium (Flanders); Northern Ireland; Norway; Spain
COVID-19 pandemic xv, 10, 42
CRC *see* Committee on the Rights of the Child (CRC)
creative approaches
  art-based 74, 86–88, *87*, *88*, **89**, 120
  author recommendations for 88, 90–91
  author's overview of 73–74
  music/movement-based 75, 78
  play-based 72–73, 74, 76–77, *77*
  storytelling and dramatisation-based 74–75, 77–81, *80*, *81*, 83, *84*, 85–86
  see also outdoor settings

D

Dalley, T. 86
deaths 43, 60
Decree on Integral Youth Care (Belgium) 34–35, 36
disabilities, children with 26, 58, 78 *see also* General Comment No. 9
discrimination 17, *18*, 20, 21, 44
due weight *see* views of children

E

Eichsteller, G. 107

F

Fawcett, M. 61
Flanders (Belgium) *see* Belgium (Flanders)

Fundación Secretariado Gitano (FSG) **6**, 7, 45–46

G

General Comments (UNCRC)
  author's overview of 2, 19–20
  capacity of young children 23–24
  participation rights of young children 20
General Comment No. 7 20, 21–22, 25, 55, 56, 120
General Comment No. 9 20, 55, 56
General Comment No. 12 20, 24, 25–26, 28, 31, 119
General Comment No. 14 20
Gradovski, M. 106
'Growing Up' agency (Belgium) 36–37

H

Holthoff, S. 107

I

image theatre 83, *84*, 85–86
infants
  behaviours 56, 57–58, 63
  mentalisation and 57–59, 60
  participation rights 56–57
  the term 'infant' 55–56
  see also best interests of children; capacities; communication; participation rights; rights; views of children; voices of children
informed consent 36
International Federation of Social Workers 2

J

Janson, S. 56

K

Kalff, Dora 76
Kennan, D. 19

Kitbag 120
Kröger, T. 78

L

Landreth, Garry 77
love 49
Lowenfeld, Margaret 76
Lundy, Laura 19, 20, 21

M

managers 8, 121–122
mentalisation 57–59, 60
mindsets *see* participatory attitudes/mindsets
Mosaic technique 81–83, *83*
Moss, P. 82
music/movement-based creative approaches 75, 78

N

NICCY 41, 42
nongovernmental organisations (NGOs) 5
nonprofit organisations 7
nonverbal communication 21, 25–26, 49, 63, 73, 86
Northern Ireland
  author's overview of 38
  child welfare challenges in 42–43
  child welfare services in 38–40
  PANDA project team 5, **6**, 7
  participation of children in 41–42
  UNCRC and 39, 41, 42
  Voice of Young People in Care (VOYPIC) 5, **6**, **42**
Northern Ireland Commission for Children and Young People (NICCY) 41, 42
Norway
  author's overview of 46–47
  child welfare challenges in 50
  child welfare services in 47–48, 99–101
  outdoor settings 98, 111
  PANDA project team 5, **6**, 7

INDEX

participation of children in 48–50
Sami people 46, 48
UNCRC and 48–50
very young children 55–56
Nupponen, A.M. 78

O

observations 61–62
outdoor settings
  activities 108–111, *110*
  author's overview of 98–99
  case studies of 102–104
  safety 111–113
  social pedagogy and 104–105, 106–107

P

PANDA project
  author's overview of 1, 4–5, 10–11
  objectives 8–9
  project team 5, **6**, 7–8
  resources by 9–10, 123
  see also Belgium (Flanders); creative approaches; Northern Ireland; Norway; participation rights; professionals; social workers; Spain
pandemic *see* COVID-19 pandemic
parents/caregivers
  capacities of 27
  due weight to, child's views 27
  mentalisation by 57–59, 60
  obligations of 25
  responsibilities of 39
  rights of 39
  support for 64
participation
  author recommendations for 65–66, **67**, 120–123
  playfulness 72–73
  process, as a 11
  social participation 44, 45–46
  supporting of very young children 57–59
  see also creative approaches; outdoor settings

participation rights
  age of children and 54–55
  author's overview of 11–13
  Belgium (Flanders), in 34–38
  challenges, contextual 42–43, 46, 50
  factors that impede 3–4
  Northern Ireland, in 41–42
  Norway 48–50
  policy recommendations 66
  resources 9–10, 123
  Spain 45–46
  UNCRC and 11, 17–19, *18*, *19*, 20–21, 54–55, 71, 119–120
  very young children 56–57
participatory attitudes/mindsets 11, 12, 22, 29, 65, 72, 121
play-based creative approaches 72–73, 74, 76–81, *77*, *80*, *81*
playfulness 72–73
policy makers 8, 122–123
power imbalances 107
professionals
  author recommendations for 65–66, **67**, 88, 90–91, 120–121
  best practice principles for 29, **30**, 31
  capacity of children 23–25
  challenges faced by 59–60
  conceptual frameworks for 57–59
  objectives for, PANDA project 8
  obligations of 25
  see also creative approaches; outdoor settings; social workers
puppets 77–81, *80*, *81*

R

Råde, A. 78
REACCH website 9
Reddick, D. 86
relational autonomy 57
research *see* PANDA project
rights
  children's under UNCRC 17–19, *18*, *19*, 20–22

competence of children, and 36
consent, and 36, 40, 48
exercising of 25
voice of the child 40, 48
see also participation rights
role playing 74
Roma people 7, 12, 43, 44–46, 121
Ruch, Gillian 7

S

Sami people 46, 48
sandplay therapy 76–77, 77
scholarship, gaps in 4
Scotland 55, 117–118, 122
Signs of Safety 37
social participation 44, 45–46
social pedagogy 90, 104, 105, 106, 107
social work 2–3
social workers
  agency of very young children, respecting 22–23
  author recommendations for 65–66, **67**, 88, 90–91
  challenges faced by 59–60
  parents/caregivers, support for 64
  playfulness 72–73
  role of 60, 61–64
  trusting relationships with children, building 71, 101, 106, 107, 120
  see also creative approaches; outdoor settings
sociology of childhood 22–23
Spain
  author's overview of 43–44
  child welfare challenges in 46
  Fundación Secretariado Gitano (FSG) **6**, 7
  PANDA project team 5, **6**, 7
  participation of children in 45–46
  Roma people 7, 12, 43, 44–46, 121
  UNCRC and 45
  very young children 56
storytelling and dramatisation-based creative approaches 74–75, 77–81, *80*, *81*, 83, *84*, 85–86
strengths-based approaches 35, 37
Sustainable Development Goals (SDGs) 3

T

theatre 74, 83, *84*, 85–86
Thrana, H.M. 86, 87, 88
toddlers 55
trainers 9, 10, 123
trusting relationships 71, 101, 106, 107, 120

U

UN SDGs (Sustainable Development Goals) 3
UNCRC (UN Convention on the Rights of the Child)
  articles of, overview of 17–19, *18*, *19*
  Belgium (Flanders), and 34–38
  Committee on the Rights of the Child (CRC) 2, 17, 19
  legal obligations under 3, 4, 10, 16–17
  Northern Ireland, and 39, 41, 42
  Norway, and 48–50
  parental/caregiver support 64
  participation rights 11, 17–19, *18*, *19*, 54–55, 71, 119–120
  rights of children 17
  Spain, and 45
  very young children 54–55, 56
  see also General Comments (UNCRC); *specific articles (for example, UNCRC Article 12)*
UNCRC Article 2 17, *18*, *19*, 20, 21
UNCRC Article 3 17, *18*, *19*, 20, 28–29
UNCRC Article 5 18, *19*, 20, 26–27
UNCRC Article 6 17, *18*, *19*
UNCRC Article 12 18, *18*, 19, *19*, 20–21, 22, 24, 28, 101, 119

INDEX

UNCRC Article 13 18, *19*
UNCRC Article 14 18, *19*
UNCRC Article 15 18, *19*
UNCRC Article 17 19, *19*
UNCRC Article 18 64
UNCRC Article 27 64
Union Internationale de la Marionnette (UNIMA) 78

V

very young children
  agency 21–22, 22–23, 57, 107
  author's overview of 2, 55–56
  deaths of 43, 60
  see also babies; best interests of children; capacities; communication; infants; participation rights; rights; views of children; voices of children
views of children
  assessment of 24–25
  best interests of children and 28–29, 49
  best practice principles for 29, **30**, 31
  due weight 18, 21, 22, 24, 25, 27–28, 101, 119
  expression of, supporting 29, **30**, 31
  formation of 24
  recognition of 25–27
Voice of Young People in Care (VOYPIC) 5, **6**, 42
voices of children
  importance of 1–2
  Mosaic technique 81–83, *83*
  power of 107
  rights, and 40, 48
  very young children 59–60, 65–66, **67**

W

Ward, C. 19
Warming, H. 102
Watson, D. 61
Winnicott, D.W. 56, 57
Winter, K. 101
World Technique 76